D0776998

God's Heart for You

Holley Gerth

HARVEST HOUSE PUBLISHERS

EUGENE, OREGON

Cover by Koechel Peterson & Associates, Inc., Minneapolis, Minnesota

Cover illustration © Hemera / Thinkstock

Holley Gerth is represented by MacGregor Literary.

GOD'S HEART FOR YOU

Copyright © 2011 by Holley Gerth
Published by Harvest House Publishers
Eugene, Oregon 97402
www.harvesthousepublishers.com

ISBN 978-0-7369-3855-6

Printed in China

11 12 13 14 15 16 17 18 19 / RDS-SK / 10 9 8 7 6 5 4 3 2

Acknowledgments

Writing a book is a journey, and I'm so grateful for the amazing traveling companions I've had along the way!

Mark, you're the love of my life and a gift from God. I'm so thankful you have your feet on the ground so I can keep my head in the clouds (and fingers on the keyboard!).

Dad and Mom, you've believed in this dream the longest and encouraged me the loudest. Thank you for your love, support, and prayers.

Poppi, this all started when I was a little girl in your Christian bookstore with you and Nana. Thanks for the seeds of faith you planted in me that have grown into the words on these pages.

Granny Eula and Grandpa Red, I appreciate your legacy of hard work and commitment—both of which I needed to complete this book.

For the rest of my family, thanks to each of you for helping me become who I am and for encouraging me along the way.

I'm also incredibly grateful to my dear friends who are a lot like family—especially our small group and the women of (in)courage. You've been God's heart to me in so many ways.

Chip MacGregor, thanks for being a fantastic agent and catching the vision. And thanks to the Harvest House team for this opportunity and your commitment to getting my words into the hands and hearts of women. I'm especially grateful for my editors, Hope Lyda and Gene Skinner.

DaySpring, I'm so glad to be partners with you in ministry and business so we can bring hope and encouragement together.

Most of all, I'm grateful to You, Lord, for loving me as I am and sharing Your heart with me so I can do the same for Your daughters. I am Your servant; may it be to me as You have said. Use me as little or as much as You desire.

Contents

Introduction

Turn on the television. Spend time on the Internet. Take a walk through your local mall. Everywhere we go there are messages about who we are and who we're supposed to be.

And yet in the middle of it all, one voice is quietly calling to our hearts.

It's the voice of the One Who Loves Us.

He whispers, "You're wanted. You matter. You're wonderfully made."

In our noisy world, our busy lives, those words that express God's heart for you can get lost. This book is an invitation to find them again.

As a writer and counselor, I connect with women each week who tell me they struggle to find their worth and purpose. I know what that's like because I've struggled with the same issues. During a season when the lies were especially loud, God prompted me to get up early each morning to spend time listening to Him. (Confession: I'm not a morning person. Once I even put chocolate on the alarm clock to bribe myself to get up. I ate the chocolate and went back to bed.) This seemed like quite a challenge, but thankfully, I decided to do it anyway.

The pages that follow contain the encouraging words I heard from God's heart in those early morning hours. These truths changed my life. I believe they'll do the same for you. Consider this your personal invitation to set aside a little time with Him. (You don't even have to get up early—although I still recommend the chocolate no matter what time you choose!) Grab a cup of coffee or tea, pick up your Bible, and just let God love on you awhile.

I'll be right beside you too.

꙳ *Holley* ꙳

PS Knowing God's heart for us begins with having a relationship with Him. If you'd like to find out more about what that means, turn to "Connecting Your Heart to God's" on page 169.

ONE

Accepted

*Accept one another, then, just as Christ
accepted you, in order to bring praise to God.*

ROMANS 15:7

It's easy for me to believe God loves me. I can understand He has forgiven me. But making the leap to
believing He has truly accepted me is another story.
Perhaps that's because we experience so little true acceptance with each other. The preacher talks about grace
but gives us a list of rules to follow. Friends promise to
always be there for us, only to turn their backs when we
don't meet their expectations. Families boast of unconditional love but withdraw it when we choose a different path. So like Adam and Eve in the Garden, we hide
from ourselves, each other, and God.

In *Beyond the Masquerade: Unveiling the Authentic
You*, Dr. Julianna Slattery says, "Facing others without
covering my psychological blemishes is actually more ter-
rifying than going out into the world without a shower or
makeup. Far more offensive than body odor are my fears,
malicious thoughts, insecurities, shame, and pride."[1]

While we strive to make ourselves acceptable, we also secretly long for someone to catch a glimpse of our true selves and exclaim, "You can stop hiding now—I really do love you just as you are!" In the Mark of the Lion trilogy by Francine Rivers, one character, Hadassah, miraculously survives an attack. However, she walks away with deep scars and always wears veils to cover them. Most of all, she fears rejection from the man she loves if he ever sees her as she truly is. This moving passage describes what happens when he finally does:

> "Oh, beloved." The wounds had been deep, the scars running from her forehead to her chin and throat. Releasing her wrists, he touched her face tenderly, tracing the mark of the lion. "You are beautiful." He cupped her head in his hands and kissed her forehead, her cheek, her chin, her mouth. "You are beautiful." She opened her eyes as he drew back slightly and he looked into them. What she saw melted all resistance, removed all shame.[2]

Those words touch our hearts because we long to hear them ourselves. Yet there is Someone who speaks this way to our hearts every day. When Christ went to the cross, He made it possible for us to stop hiding. All of our sin, shame, and guilt have been erased. The Lord constantly looks at us with eyes of love. His scars bring healing and even beauty to our own.

Will the Lord still reveal areas in our lives that need to change? Yes, of course. But His conviction is about *what we do*, not *who we are*. Real friends tell you when you have something in your teeth. They love you enough to speak the truth, and Jesus is our most faithful friend of all. He sees deep within our hearts and tells us when something is stuck there that doesn't belong. His correction always comes with grace, not condemnation.

When we open our hearts and let God speak to us, we discover, like Hadassah, that we're truly known and loved in a way we never thought possible. The acceptance we long for is already ours if only we'll dare to embrace it.

You are accepted.

Reflect

Read Romans 15:1-7. Complete this sentence: Being accepted means that I…

How is conviction different from condemnation?

What helps you believe God truly accepts you?

Respond

Lord, I'm so grateful You love and accept me just as I am. Sometimes that truth is hard to understand and embrace, so I pray You'll help me learn to walk fully in it. I thank You for showing my heart…

Hey you,
the one wondering if you're enough,
if you'd be loved if anyone really knew you—
turn your heart this way for a moment,
then lean in and listen close…
Acceptance?
You've got it.
You don't have to look any further
than the hands of the One who made you,
the heart of the One who loves you.
You're welcomed, held,
cherished just as you are
and encouraged to grow
into all you'll become.
So hold your heart and head high;
look the world in the eyes and say…
"I'm His. I'm loved.
I'm already accepted today."

TWO

Wonderfully Made

I praise You because
I am fearfully and wonderfully made;
Your works are wonderful,
I know that full well.

PSALM 139:14

Where something is made matters to us. Look at the tag on most any product and you'll likely see a line like these imprinted on it:

MADE IN CHINA

MADE IN MEXICO

MADE IN AMERICA

And if you could see the line imprinted on your heart, it would read, MADE IN HEAVEN. The word *made* usually conjures up visions of factories and impersonal production lines, but the way heaven creates is entirely different. Every part of you was carefully and intricately crafted by God. Of course, that creation was carried out physically in your mother's womb, but the idea of you started in the heart of heaven itself.

Since the beginning of the world, God has been

creating. The word *made* appears ten times in the first two chapters of Genesis. God made light, stars, animals, and finally His crowning creation—people. When He finished, "God saw all that he had made, and it was very good" (Genesis 1:31). What He said over all creation, I believe He said at your birth too: "It is very good." That statement isn't a reflection of your morality or what other people say about you. It really isn't about you at all. Instead, it's the expression of the Master Craftsman looking at His work and declaring its worth.

We often fail to agree with God's assessment of us. With our words and actions, we fill in the blanks in other ways. Instead of "It is good," we look in the mirror and say, "It is ugly. It is unlovable. It is worthless."

In 1987 a British couple brought a painting to *Antiques Roadshow* to find out its value. They didn't particularly like it and had actually moved it to a shed when they redecorated. Imagine their surprise when the painting turned out to be *The Halt in the Desert* by Richard Dard, a well-known artist. The painting had been missing for 100 years, and its value (£100,000, or about $150,000 today) set a record on the show.[3] It didn't matter what the couple thought about the piece; its value came from the one who created it.

You and I are works of a master artist as well. We may hide who we truly are and display to the world something we think is more appealing. We may dip our brushes into the paint and cover ourselves with another image. We may even seek to destroy ourselves completely out of shame. But the truth still remains—we are fearfully and wonderfully made.

Max Lucado says in *Cure for the Common Life*, "Da Vinci painted one Mona Lisa. Beethoven composed one Fifth Symphony. And God made one version of you...We exist to exhibit God, to display His glory. We serve as canvases for His brushstroke, papers for His pen, soil for His seeds, glimpses of His image."[4]

God longs for His children to embrace the worth and value He's given them and then use it to bless others. When we know who we are and whose we are, we're free to love, live with joy, and make a difference in the world.

You are wonderfully made.

Reflect

Read Psalm 139. What has influenced your self-image, both positively and negatively?

What's one truth your heart needs to remember about who you are as God's creation?

Write down one small way you can begin living more fully in that truth today.

Respond

Lord, I praise You because I am fearfully and wonderfully made. Help me to see myself as You see
me, the creation of the Master Artist who lovingly
chose each detail of who I am. I thank You for
making me…

You're formed by God's hands,
dreamed up in His heart,
and placed in this world for a purpose.
There's no one else like you…
You're one of a kind, irreplaceable.
God has given you everything you need
and created you just as you need to be
to make a difference
in your own wonderful way.
So go for it, girl.
*The world is waiting
and heaven is cheering you on.*

THREE

Forgiven

If you, O LORD, kept a record of sins...
who could stand?
But with you there is forgiveness.

PSALM 130:3-4

I messed up. Again. I sat on the back deck thinking about what a failure I'd been. What must God think of me? I was writing in my journal as I had been every day. Lately, I felt God had been impressing on me to only write good things—compliments people gave me, ways He used me, blessings in my life. I didn't know why He wanted me to do this, but I felt compelled to do it. But on this morning I sat and stared at the blank page. I began to write about my mistake. I finished and looked at the black and white evidence that I was a failure yet again.

Then I seemed to hear a whisper in my heart. "Rip out the page."

I paused and listened closer. "Rip out the page."

"God, what are You saying? What do You mean, rip out the page? I need to record this mistake. I need to remember it."

Again the clear message came. "Rip out the page."

I touched the white page of my journal, now covered with writing. Then slowly I pulled from top to bottom. The paper made a sharp sound as it separated from the journal. Only a few fragments of white paper remained where my mistake once had been. The picture couldn't have been clearer.

Forgiveness. Mercy. Grace. They were right there on the clean, white pages of my journal.

God seemed to whisper to my heart again. "All of the mistakes and failures you remember, all the secrets you run from, all the regrets and remorse…they are all gone. Every one of them has been torn from the story of your life. You are forgiven. You are accepted. You are loved." My heart was overwhelmed.

I kept thinking about what God had spoken to me on the deck. Later in the morning, I prayed about it again. This time I sensed God adding something more to what He had whispered.

Daughter, do you know why I wanted you to keep a "good things" journal? It's because that's what My journal about you is like. If you were to read the story of your life, that's what you would read. Not mistakes or failures, but the times you were a blessing, the ways you please Me, the love you show others. The good things I think about you.

God's love was so real and strong, so much bigger than I even imagined. I realized at that moment that God loves me. He doesn't just tolerate me. He doesn't just put up with me because I'm a Christian and He has to. He really, truly loves me.

So wherever you are, whatever mistake you have written in the journal of your life, know that God has ripped it from the pages. There's only love. There's only grace. The story of your life is far different than you imagined…and the Author loves you far more than you ever dared to dream.

You are forgiven.

Reflect

Read Psalm 130. Search your heart. Is there anything you believe God can't or won't forgive?

How does your heart feel different on the days when you live in forgiveness and grace?

If God wrote a journal about your life, what do you think it might say?

Respond

Lord, I confess to You that I…

and I receive Your forgiveness. I'm so glad my sins are gone and I'm in a right relationship with You! Amen.

⸺

You really are *forgiven*,
slate-wiped-clean,
sins-washed-away,
brand new.
All those mistakes,
all that pain,
there's only
one thing that remains…
grace
full and free,
deeper than the sea,
wide enough to
wrap its arms
around you and
draw you close to His heart—
the place where you've always belonged.

FOUR

Loved

God is love... There is no fear in love.
But perfect love drives out fear, because
fear has to do with punishment. The one
who fears is not made perfect in love.

1 JOHN 4:16,18

Fil Anderson knows what it's like to live in fear. For years he felt driven to earn God's approval. That drive took him all the way to the door of a psychiatric unit, where he got his first glimpse of grace. Yet as soon as he left, the old patterns began again. Serving as a pastor only further drained him as he told others about the love of God and yet often felt as if he could never experience it himself. He reflects on this in his book *Running on Empty: Contemplative Spirituality for Overachievers*.

> My default nature is set to believe that God's acceptance, love, and care for me is directly proportional to my level of activity for God. This

belief system—the more I do for God, the more God will love me—has dictated my every waking activity more than anything else. And it has threatened to starve my soul.[5]

Fil lived in fear of what God would do unless he earned His approval. When Fil discovered unconditional love, his world changed forever. He says, "Nothing I am capable of doing will ever cause God to love me more...And nothing I ever do will cause God to love me less. That idea used to sound like madness to me. Then I realized that, in a way, it *is* madness."[6] God's extravagant love makes no sense to us because we try to make it about us. We compare it to human love, which is conditional. So we try to earn, deserve, or win it in some way. But God's love is different from ours. God doesn't just give love—He *is* love.

As women, we are experts at earning the affections of friends, lovers, children, and our families. Coming face-to-face with a God who loves us unconditionally sets us off balance. It's much easier to believe, "If I go to church and read my Bible, God will love me." That makes us feel safe because it seems we can control God's love. It's scary to believe in God's unconditional love. What if it's not true? Then the deepest desire of every little girl and grown woman can never be a reality. We watch Cinderella and hope for our own version of living happily ever after. But life disappoints us, and God is our last chance to be fully, deeply loved. So we do everything possible to please Him because even though we've endured many rejections, His would be unbearable.

But God is whispering the words to our hearts we long to hear if only we can dare to believe them: "You are loved—deeply, truly, always." That's the kind of crazy love that set Fil Anderson free, and it's ours as well. God invites us to take His hand, trust His heart, and believe that the love we've been searching for all our lives is the love we've already found.

You are loved.

Reflect

Read 1 John 4:13-21. Who has influenced your view of God's love for you?

How is God's love different from human love?

Describe a time in your life when you sensed God's love for you.

Respond

Lord, Your unconditional love for me is more than my human heart can completely comprehend. I pray You will lead me into more of Your love and open my eyes to truly see it. I ask for Your help to…

Step outside for a moment.
Let's look up at the infinite blue.
That's how much God loves you.
For as high as the heavens are above the earth,
so great is His love for those
who fear him (Psalm 103:11).
When's the last time the sky got lower?
Oh, sure, the clouds come in…
busy days, hard times, storms.
But they're only illusions
because the sky stays just as high.
Regardless of how it seems,
Regardless of what we do,
It's the same when it comes to His love for you.
It's never any less, never any lower.
It remains steady, constant, endless as the heavens.
So tell your heart this secret:
His love won't let you down.
And anytime you need to remember that's true…
just look up.

FIVE

Blessed

*Praise be to the God and Father of our Lord
Jesus Christ, who has blessed us in the heavenly
realms with every spiritual blessing in Christ.*

EPHESIANS 1:3

B less you!"
  "Let's say the blessing."
  "Bless your heart."
"God bless America."

The word *bless* has become part of our everyday language. We look at it casually, almost like a slightly more spiritual version of a wish. Even those with highly sensitive radar for political correctness can accept the word *bless*. Yet this word began as much more than a desire for well-being in another person or nation. Rolf Garborg explains in his book *The Family Blessing*.

Throughout the Bible we find ample evidence that the God of Abraham was a God of blessing. In fact, the words *bless* or *blessing* appear in Scripture in some form or another about seven hundred times. Apparently Abraham, along with countless other people in the Bible, needed and welcomed the grace, power, and encouragement that could be poured into their lives through God's blessing.[7]

The first blessing appears in Genesis 1:22: "God blessed them and said, 'Be fruitful and increase in number.'" This type of blessing is yours simply because you exist. All of humanity experiences God's goodness in many ways. As Jesus said, "[God] causes his sun to rise on the evil and the good" (Matthew 5:45).

For those of us who are in Christ, the blessings go much deeper and include the spiritual blessings of heaven. Ephesians 1:3 makes an astounding claim— every spiritual blessing is ours through Christ. God has not withheld anything from us. Grace, peace, hope, love, strength…they are all ours.

A local legend tells of a man who lived in poverty for years on a farm. He spent his days desperately trying to make a living from his land. Then one day an oil company came calling. He agreed to let them drill, and within a few months he was a millionaire.

The blessings in our lives are much the same way. They are already waiting beneath the surface. Like the oil company, the Holy Spirit reveals our blessings and helps us draw them out. Jesus promised that the Spirit would guide us into all truth (John 16:13). As long as we live like the farmer and try to get by on our own strength, the deepest blessings will elude us. Only as we yield to the Spirit and let Him drill deeper and deeper into our lives will we uncover all that is truly ours.

Blessings can come through happy or hard times. And after they're revealed, we need to protect them. The enemy comes to steal and kill and destroy (John 10:10), and he would like nothing better than to siphon off what is ours. The process of receiving and protecting our blessings will continue until it is complete in heaven.

Next time you hear someone casually exclaim, "Bless you!" take a moment to pause and remember you are already blessed. Far more than you could ever ask or imagine has been given to you through Christ. You are spiritually rich beyond your wildest dreams. Our heavenly Father held nothing back from us—may nothing hold us back from living fully in His blessings.

You are blessed.

Reflect

Read Ephesians 1:1-14. What is a blessing?

List a few of the blessings you're grateful God has given you.

What's one simple way you can share God's blessings with someone else today?

Respond

Lord, I'm grateful for all that is mine through Christ, and I'm still realizing how truly blessed I am in You. I deeply appreciate…

⁓

You are blessed,
not just with what you need for today
but with everything that matters for all eternity.
You are blessed,
not just with good things
but with the best of all God has to offer.
You are blessed,
not just because you're alive
but because you're loved by One who's Life Himself.
You are blessed,
not just so you can receive
but so you can give and be a blessing too
(and you are).

SIX

Chosen

*You are a chosen people, a royal priesthood, a
holy nation, a people belonging to God, that
you may declare the praises of him who called
you out of darkness into his wonderful light.*

1 PETER 2:9

Imagine a little girl at recess waiting to hear her name
called for a team. She stands with her head lowered,
staring at a scuffed shoe, waiting and hoping. Picture a woman lingering at the edge of a party. Her eyes
scan the room, wondering if anyone notices she's there,
silently wishing for someone to talk to her. See an older
lady sitting in the foyer of a nursing home. She watches
as volunteers come through the door, slowly lifting her
head, inviting someone to acknowledge her with a
quiet smile. From the time we are children to the end
of our lives, something within us cries, "Choose me!"

Jesus answers that call of our hearts. He says to the
little girl, "I want you on My team. I even have a special
position and purpose for you." He says to the woman
at the party, "I think you're beautiful. I want to know
you and be with you." He says to the older woman, "I

place great worth on your life. I see you and I hear you." And He says to you, "I choose you just as you are, and I love you more than you can imagine."

As a child, I loved the musical *Annie*. It tells the story of an eleven-year-old orphan who is stuck in an orphanage run by the cruel Miss Hannigan. Annie is selected to be adopted by Daddy Warbucks, an incredibly wealthy man. At first Annie and Daddy Warbucks don't get along, but they grow to have a deep bond and love for each other. However, Annie still insists that her real parents will come for her, and she searches for them. A couple eventually comes forward, but it's later revealed that they only claimed Annie for financial gain and that her real parents are no longer living. Daddy Warbucks rescues Annie from harm, and the two of them become a family for good.

Annie ran for almost six years on Broadway, it won the Tony Award for best musical, and it was made into a popular movie. Perhaps *Annie* enjoyed such success because we all feel a bit like her at times. At one point Annie says, "I didn't want to be just another orphan, Mr. Warbucks. I wanted to believe I was special." We long for someone to come for us, see us for who we really are, and want us anyway. Like Annie, we've already been chosen, but sometimes we still try to fulfill that longing in other ways. Eventually we find, as she did, that the love we've been searching for is right in front of us.

God has already made His decision. He's standing before us with arms wide open. Once and for all He has said to us, "I choose you." When we accept our heavenly Father's invitation to join His family, we truly belong to Him forever.

You are chosen.

Reflect

Read 1 Peter 2:4-10. What does it mean to you to be chosen by God?

What lies might keep you from fully believing He has chosen you?

What is a truth your heart can hold on to today?

Respond

Lord, I'm so thankful You chose me. My heart is Yours, and today I want You to know…

We live in a world of want ads.
Some of them are printed on pages;
many more are unspoken.

Wanted:

A woman who is a perfect friend,
mom, wife, coworker,
housekeeper, cook, driver, thinker,
encourager, and more.
Messy, real, in-progress people need not apply.
God has a very different idea in mind.

Wanted:

A woman who is imperfect, in need of grace,
gloriously gifted, flawed, and beautiful
and who dares to believe she's loved through it all
by a God who has an amazing purpose for her life.
No need to apply.
You've already been chosen.

SEVEN

Free

*You, my brothers, were called to be free. But
do not use your freedom to indulge the sinful
nature; rather, serve one another in love.*

GALATIANS 5:13

Dorothy Still Danner knew the value of freedom.
As a Navy nurse in World War II, she witnessed
firsthand the destruction of Pearl Harbor. She
also spent from 1942 to 1945 as a prisoner of war in the
Philippines. While she was held captive with more than
3000 others, conditions grew worse and food became
scarce. In a daring operation, American soldiers over-
took the camp where the prisoners were held. Dorothy says of her rescuers, "Oh, we never saw anything so
handsome in our lives."[8]

We may never face anything like Dorothy did, but
we all know what it's like to be held captive by something. It might be a negative attitude. Perhaps an addiction. Or maybe a destructive relationship. We're not
confined by physical walls but rather trapped within
our minds, waiting to be rescued. When Dorothy had

the opportunity to be liberated, she joyfully welcomed it. She returned home as a hero to share the rest of her life with those she loved. If someone asked her if she would like to return to the camp and become a prisoner again, undoubtedly the answer would be a firm and insistent no!

We have also been set free through Christ, and yet many times we stay in bondage. We might be like prisoners of war who simply didn't realize the war had already been won and remained in captivity when victory was already theirs. Perhaps we have been imprisoned for so long that we just can't imagine any other life. Our situation may be difficult, but at least it's familiar and predictable. Or we might fear that God isn't really our ally and try to rescue ourselves instead of letting Him set us free. Whatever our reason, we are not made to be in bondage, and our hearts will be restless until we find true freedom.

For Dorothy, true freedom meant being able to go home to her friends and family. It meant good meals, hot showers, and a safe haven. It meant regaining the ability to pursue her dreams and live without fear. For those of us who serve Christ, freedom means being able to give and receive love. It means embracing grace and passing it on to others. It means following God's path and purpose for our lives rather than being held captive by fear.

Freedom does not mean doing whatever we want

to do. That's simply another form of bondage. Instead, freedom comes when we offer ourselves fully to God. The more completely we submit to His love, the freer our hearts become. We move from the prison camp to His house, where He gives us the hope, peace, and joy we need.

Dorothy Still Danner never forgot the price paid for her freedom. Two soldiers willingly lost their lives so the prisoners could regain theirs. The Son of God paid the same price for us. Now He says to each of our hearts, "Come and enjoy the freedom I have gained for you. The battle has been fought, the victory has been won, and love is waiting for you to come home."

You are free.

Reflect

Read Galatians 5:13-26. Complete this sentence: Freedom is...

How free does your heart feel right now? Why?

What helps you protect the freedom that is yours through Christ?

Respond

Lord, thank You so much for my freedom. I choose to submit to Your love and lordship. Please show me any areas where I am still in bondage and set me free with Your truth. I'm so grateful for the way You've freed me from…

You're released from chains,
out of bondage,
brought into wide-open spaces.
Nothing can keep you down,
hold you back,
or tie you up.
You're free.
So spread your wings,
daughter of His,
feel the wind in your hair,
His love on your face.
Then stretch out your heart
and soar.

EIGHT

Provided For

Give us each day our daily bread.

LUKE 11:3

I woke this morning dreaming of big, delicious cupcakes with thick frosting and cream filling. You know the kind. My mind must have fixated on that goodness after reading the history of Sprinkles Cupcakes for the first time.[9]

Here's my favorite part of the Sprinkles Cupcakes story. One of the reasons Candace Nelson started the company was simply so she could bring joy to others. Sweet success soon followed.

And as I read this Scripture passage this morning, right in the middle of Christ's words, a new lightbulb came on in my heart about bringing joy to others too.

Jesus tells a parable about a guy whose friend comes to town unexpectedly. He has nothing to feed his guest, so he goes to his neighbor and asks for bread. At first, the neighbor whines about it being late at night, but the guy keeps on banging and eventually gets the bread. The whole point of the parable is that if a cranky neighbor will give you bread when you ask, how much more will the God who deeply loves you do the same—and give you even more than you need.

But this morning I noticed something for the first time. The guy was asking for bread for someone else, not for himself. And he says three little words that caught me by surprise: "I have nothing." Insecurity prompts us to say those words too, doesn't it? But having nothing didn't stop this man. In fact, it provided a reason to make a request.

What if we responded that way too? Someone needs bread—perhaps physically, or maybe emotionally or spiritually. Yet we feel we have nothing to offer. And really, apart from Christ, that's true. But we aren't apart from Him, ever. And we have limitless access to all of His resources. So God invites us to ask for bread on behalf of ourselves and each other. And to ask boldly, persistently.

"Give us each day our daily bread," goes the line in the Lord's Prayer. What if that bread isn't just for us? What if it's for someone else too? Either way, all we have to do is ask. The answer may not be what we have in mind, but we can trust it will always come from a God who loves us.

I've decided I'm not just asking for any ol' bread if I'm talking to the limitless God of the universe, who promises to provide for us. I'm doing a little dreaming and asking for cupcakes (aka joy) to pass around—big, delicious ones with pink frosting and cream filling. You know the kind.

You are provided for.

Reflect

Read Luke 11:1-10. What does your heart need from God today?

What might someone else in your life need from you?

Describe a time God provided for you.

Respond

Lord, I praise You for not only providing for my needs but also using me to help meet the needs of others too. Today I humbly ask You for...

Taste and see
that the Lord is good to you.
He provides for all your needs.
Daily bread.
Manna.
The here-and-now truth your soul craves.
The forever grace your heart needs.
He is the God of the everyday,
the practical, the ordinary.
And of the eternal, the intangible,
the beyond-your-imagination.
He is limitless in His love for you.
His provision in your life will be too.

NINE

Enough

His divine power has given us everything
we need for life and godliness
through our knowledge of him.

2 PETER 1:3

A woman sat quietly in my counseling office with tears streaming down her face. All of her life she had been told lies that ended with one word—*enough*. "You're not good enough…smart enough…pretty enough." Her father was impossible to please. Her husband followed suit. As a result she worked harder and harder, burying her emotions deeper within and hoping that one day she could earn acceptance. As we prayed together and she renounced some of the lies she had believed about herself, I sensed the Lord whispering to my heart one simple sentence over and over. *Tell her she is enough.*

After we said "amen," I took a deep breath, looked at her, and quietly said, "You are enough. All of your life people have made you feel as if you are not. But that's a lie. I think God wants you to know that you are enough, just as you are." When I spoke those words it was as if a dam broke within her. Rather than gently slipping down her face, the tears began to pour out from a place she had kept locked for years. When she finally looked up, she wore a bright smile as if a load had been lifted from her shoulders.

As I drove home that night, I wondered at God's grace. I began to think, "If He wanted to say that to her, then perhaps He wants to say it to me as well." Like most women, I relentlessly push myself to be and do more. Deep inside, I also live with the lie that says *I am not enough*. As I pondered and prayed, the Lord began to reveal more about this truth. Being enough in God's kingdom does not mean having status, wealth, or stunning beauty. It's an entirely different perspective from what the world sees as enough. In God's eyes, *we are enough because He is enough*. When we give our lives to Christ, we become new creations (2 Corinthians 5:17). We also gain access to all He has to offer and have "everything we need for life and godliness."

Jesus shared this truth in a parable when He said, "I am the vine; you are the branches. If a man remains in me and I in him, he will bear much fruit; apart from me you can do nothing" (John 15:5). Imagine a branch straining to produce fruit on its own. It tries different agricultural techniques. It goes to fruit-bearing workshops. It tries to look better than all the other branches.

But deep inside it despairs, "I am not enough." Then one day the branch connects to the vine. In this relationship, everything changes. Suddenly the way the branch has been created makes sense. It has everything it needs to fulfill its purpose. It also has every resource necessary for bearing glorious, beautiful fruit. In every way that matters, it is enough.

Like the woman in my office, we all get disconnected from the vine at times. We feel as if we have to strive for love and acceptance. Yet God invites us to come to Him and believe that no matter what the world may try to tell us, no matter which lies have wounded our hearts, no matter how inadequate we may feel at times, we are enough.

You are enough.

Reflect

Read 2 Peter 1:3-11. In what ways have you tried to earn love or acceptance?

What does God freely offer you instead?

What is He speaking to your heart today?

Respond

Lord, thank You that I am enough because You are enough. You have created me and given me everything I need to fulfill Your purpose for my life. I'm so grateful to know…

⁓

We tell ourselves, *"It's all too much."*
Then there's an answer, deep within,
calling first for all who are weary to come
and then reminding us gently…
I AM.
Because in the middle of our circumstances…
the ticking of the clock,
the spinning of the wheels,
there is one deepest fear.
It's that we won't be enough;
we'll falter under the weight of it all.
And if we do, we won't be loved.
Yes? You've heard that too?
Friend, it isn't true.
Hear words of grace instead…
You are enough in Him
because He is enough in you.

TEN

Secure

*I give them eternal life, and they shall never
perish; no one can snatch them out of my hand.*

JOHN 10:28

A typical conversation between my sweet dad and
me:

"What are you going to do tonight, Holley?"

"I'm going to clean the kitchen and go to bed."

"Well, goodnight. Be careful."

Regardless of what I'm doing, my Dad's last two
words to me are usually "Be careful." I smile whenever he says it, and I appreciate his tender and protec-
tive heart. I've also realized my heavenly Father does
not often speak those same words to me. Instead He
says, "Deny yourself…Do not fear…Be courageous."
If Christ is any example of how God treats His children (and of course He is), being careful doesn't seem
to enter into the equation much!

God has good plans for us—but He also has dan-
gerous adventures that may cost us our lives and most
certainly will cost us ourselves. John Piper said, "Risk is

right."[10] There is a time and place for safety and caution. But there is also a time to battle giants, overcome obstacles, and take leaps of faith we never thought possible.

We can do so because God is totally devoted to our security. As Jesus says in John 10, no one can snatch you out of His hand. The enemy may try to tell you that isn't true, but God never lies. Once we give our hearts to Him, we are His forever. The apostle Paul makes this as clear as he can.

> Who shall separate us from the love of Christ? Shall trouble or hardship or persecution or famine or nakedness or danger or sword? As it is written: "For your sake we face death all day long; we are considered as sheep to be slaughtered." No, in all these things we are more than conquerors through him who loved us. For I am convinced that neither death nor life, neither angels nor demons, neither the present nor the future, nor any powers, neither height nor depth, nor anything else in all creation, will be able to separate us from the love of God that is in Christ Jesus our Lord (Romans 8:35-39).

Paul faced jail, beatings, and ultimately martyrdom. Most of us will never have our safety threatened as he did. Yet he was willing to go through it all because he knew no one and nothing could take away what mattered most.

God may never ask us to face some of the challenges Paul did, but He still calls us to step out of our comfort zones and take risks for Him. That might mean reaching out to a hurting friend, beginning a new career, standing up for our beliefs, or laying down an old habit that gave us a false sense of security.

It's still hard for me to be brave sometimes. But I'm slowly learning that each of us must listen to our heavenly Father's voice. What we hear may surprise, challenge, and stretch us, but we can trust it always comes from a heart of love.

You are secure.

Reflect

Read John 10:7-30. How is safety different from security?

Which one do you think it's easier to focus on? Why?

How might God be asking you to step out of your comfort zone today?

Respond

Lord, thank You that I am eternally secure in You. No matter how I feel or what may happen, that

will always be true. Help me to fully live in that
reality today. I ask for the courage to...

In this world of "maybe" and "might"
and "I changed my mind"
there's One whose YES
is as certain as the sun,
as solid as a rock.
You can build your life on it,
rest your heart in it.
And you can take that step,
make that leap,
dare to live that dream
because Someone Who Loves You
is holding you up
and will never let you down.

ELEVEN

Called

Think of what you were when you were called.

1 CORINTHIANS 1:26

In the movie *The Princess Diaries*, Mia Thermopolis (Anne Hathaway) is an awkward teenager enduring the usual difficulties of high school. That all changes the day her paternal grandmother Clarisse Renaldi (Julie Andrews) arrives with shocking news. It turns out that Mia is far from ordinary. She is, in fact, a princess and the only heir to the throne of Genovia. Mia proceeds to get herself into a series of mishaps and embarrassing situations as she seeks to become the person she rightfully already is. In the end, Mia decides to accept the position of princess even though she doesn't feel qualified. She has the courage to say yes only after she reads the heartfelt letter from her father, the former king, written to her before his death.

We'll probably never be called to rule a country, but we all have a moment when the King of kings calls us to be a princess in His kingdom. Much like Mia, we may initially respond, "Who, me?" The apostle Paul puts it this way:

Think of what you were when you were called. Not many of you were wise by human standards; not many were influential; not many were of noble birth. But God chose the foolish things of the world to shame the wise; God chose the weak things of the world to shame the strong. He chose the lowly things of this world and the despised things—and the things that are not—to nullify the things that are, so that no one may boast before him (1 Corinthians 1:26-29).

In other words, our calling isn't about us. Like Mia, we may not see ourselves as princess material, but what matters most is the will of our Father.

Even after we've accepted God's offer to be a princess, we may forget our calling from time to time. Imagine if Mia moved out of the palace and lived on the streets. Her beautiful gowns would become dirty, she would have little to eat, and few would guess her real identity. Yet the fact that she was royalty wouldn't change. Being called is just the first step. Carrying out our calling is a lifetime pursuit.

Living out our calling can sometimes be a challenge because our culture tends to confuse a calling with a vocation. We say pastors are called to the ministry. A missionary might be called overseas. Yet Scripture talks about our calling in a much deeper way. Being called by God is about *who we are* and not simply *what we do*.

You can carry out your calling as a stay-at-home mom, a CEO, a marketing director, a caregiver, or any number of other roles. What matters most is embracing your identity in Christ and living your faith wherever you are today. As Mia finally discovered, being a princess doesn't require a castle, fancy gowns, or lavish parties. It only requires a heart fully committed to the king.

You are called.

Reflect

Read 1 Corinthians 1:18-31. Describe how your relationship with God began.

How has your commitment to Him changed your life?

What is one way God is asking you to live out your calling right where you are?

Respond

Lord, I'm so glad You called me and made me part of Your kingdom. My heart wants to respond by…

Ring, ring.
There's a call for your heart.
It's been there since the day you were born.
And it will be there until
the day you go Home.
Pick it up, listen closely, and you'll hear
the voice of your Father
whispering what's true…
"You are mine.
I made you.
Chose you.
Called you.
That call isn't about a vocation.
It's about *making a difference wherever you are.*
It's about *being who I created you to be.*
No one else can take your place.
No one else can answer this call.
I'm so glad you did.
I'll be right here telling you
all you need to know
every day, every step of the way.
I love to hear your voice…
and I love when you listen to Mine."

TWELVE

Empowered

*I pray also that the eyes of your heart may be
enlightened in order that you may know…
his incomparably great power for us who
believe. That power is like the working of his
mighty strength, which he exerted in Christ
when he raised him from the dead and seated
him at his right hand in the heavenly realms.*

EPHESIANS 1:18-20

A hurricane recently left my parents without power for a few days. They live close to the Texas coast, so such happenings aren't really unusual. My mom even enjoys the way all of the neighbors gather outside each evening to entertain themselves by swapping stories and catching up on each other's lives. Yet despite their attempts to make the most of it, a hopeful question is always floating through the air: When will the power come back on?

Ever since the first lightbulb illuminated a dark space, we've made electricity an intricate part of our lives. When a region loses power for a significant amount of time, the government declares a state of emergency. Everyday activities come to a halt until the electricity crackles to life again. Headlines read, "60,000 people still without power." We all gasp and wonder what we would do if that happened to us.

In much the same way, we can also lose spiritual power in our lives. The power may go down after an emotional storm. Winds of bitterness can destroy the lines of connection between a heart and God. Or we just may not be aware of the power available to each of us when we come to know Christ. In one way or another, we all find ourselves in the dark at times.

But the power that is ours through Christ is limitless and indestructible. If it were converted into electricity, it could light the world for all eternity. The apostle Paul compares the power within us to the power God used to raise Christ from the dead and seat Him in heaven. That's not a little lightbulb. That's not even a generator. It's beyond nuclear—it's spectacular. Unparalleled in all of the universe. Nothing can extinguish it.

Our culture often talks about empowering people. That usually means giving them rights, providing opportunities, or offering education...things that come from the outside. Yet God is the greatest Empowerer of all, and He starts with the heart. He doesn't say, "Here's a little power for you, and some for you, and a bit more for you." Instead, God places all of His power within us.

What an amazing, indescribable reality—beyond our comprehension!

God expects us to use His power for His purposes. We can't simply say, "I'm going to use the power of God to leap over buildings in a single bound, clean my house in two minutes, and get that job I've always wanted." There is a catch. It only works when we're relying on Him and pursuing His will. Like a cord plugged into an outlet, the current starts flowing when there's an intimate connection. When that happens, nothing can stop what He wants to do in and through us.

You're God's powerhouse. Go light the world in your own wonderful way.

You are empowered.

Reflect

Read Ephesians 1:15-23. How would you define true power—the kind you'd like to have in your everyday life?

What helps you live fully in the power God has placed within you?

What's one way God is asking you to shine for Him today?

Respond

Lord, I'm amazed at the power You have placed within me. Help me to shine right where I am by…

⌒

Hey, you.
Yep, you.
The one feeling a little weary.
Carrying that load.
Fighting this battle.
You're beautiful, you know that?
It's true.
And you can do this with Him.
With His power.
I know it.
I feel it.
Keep going, girl.
You feel like your strength is small.
But it's not.
It's BIG.
World-changing big.
Life-altering big.
Make-it-over-that-mountain big.
BIG enough for you to do what you need to do.
Because your strength is as big as the God in you.

THIRTEEN

Irreplaceable

God has arranged the parts in the body, every
one of them, just as he wanted them to be.

1 CORINTHIANS 12:18

A friend of mine and I recently talked about how we both felt guilty for not being more like each other. I lamented to her, "I wish I could cook like you and make my house cozy like yours!" She also saw some qualities and skills in me she'd like to have. Next time we chatted, we both laughed and shook our heads at our silly comparison game. But it reminded us that it's easy to lose sight of God's heart and His unique purpose for each of us.

As women, it seems we often compare ourselves to each other. If someone is gifted in different ways than we are, we feel inadequate and wish we could change. Perhaps some of that perspective is encouraged by our individualistic society. We believe that one person could (and should) do it all. But God has a completely different plan. Rather than making each of us self-sufficient, He places us within the body of Christ with a specific role to fulfill. "If the whole body were an eye, where would the sense of hearing be? If the whole body were an ear, where would the sense of smell be?" (1 Corinthians 12:17).

People who lose limbs often experience phantom pains. The body of Christ experiences something similar when we withdraw because we don't think we matter. And this isn't about going to church—it's about sharing ourselves and our lives with others. We may think, "They don't need me. Sally is so much more creative. Alison is so much better with kids. Hannah is a much better speaker." Meanwhile, other women are probably thinking the same about us! When someone excels where we struggle, it doesn't mean we need to change or withdraw. It simply means she may have a different role in the body than we do. But whatever our role is, the body of Christ needs us and feels a loss when we're not there.

I feel at home with words, but put me in a kitchen and I'm a bit lost. My mother-in-law, Marsha, is an amazing cook. Watching her create a meal is like seeing Da Vinci paint. She flows in that element, and the results leave us all happy and satisfied. When my husband and I married, I thought, "I need to be more like Marsha!" One day the Lord impressed on me that it was okay to simply support my mother-in-law in her gifts. I appreciate who God has made her, and I try to help her when I can (even if that simply means I just peel a few potatoes). I admire the ways Marsha takes excellent care of whatever God entrusts to her. Whether it's a meal, her home, or those she loves, that's her mission.

In *Cure for the Common Life*, Max Lucado says, "With God, every day matters, every person counts. And that includes you. You do something no one else does, in a manner no one else does it. And when your uniqueness meets God's purpose, both of you will rejoice."[11] Those around you will rejoice too. The body of Christ needs you, just as you are, and no one can take your place.

You are irreplaceable.

Reflect

Read 1 Corinthians 12. In what areas do you tend to compare yourself with others?

What strengths and gifts has God given you?

Describe a time when one of your strengths or gifts helped someone else.

Respond

Lord, thank You for creating me in a wonderful way and giving me a unique purpose to fulfill. I pray You will help me use the gifts and strengths You've given me to honor You and bless others. I want to do so today by…

The world gets only one *you*.
You with your gifts.
You with your smile.
You with those things you do.
So take your place,
take your chances,
take this moment to know…
you've got something to offer.
Something good and right and true.
Something God-given,
Heart-of-heaven created.
And the rest of us need it, need *you*.
Oh, you think it's no big deal.
Anyone could be that way.
Anyone could do it.
Nope.
Not true.
There's just one *irreplaceable you*.

FOURTEEN

Known

*The LORD does not look at the things
man looks at. Man looks at the outward
appearance, but the LORD looks at the heart.*

1 SAMUEL 16:7

The average American lives within 50 miles of the town where she grew up.[12] The theme song to the hit television show *Cheers* describes a place where everybody knows your name. When we walk into a new situation, we usually scan the room quickly and wonder, "Does anyone here know me?" Being known makes us feel safe, accepted, and affirmed.

This type of knowing is mostly on the surface. People might indeed know our names, what we do for a living, or even what we were like as kids. But God says He knows us in a much deeper and more powerful way. In the Old Testament, saying someone knew his wife was a polite and powerful way of describing their physical relationship. True knowing is about deep, personal intimacy. King David marveled at God's knowledge of him in Psalm 139.

O LORD, you have searched me and you know me. You know when I sit and when I rise; you perceive my thoughts from afar. You discern my going out and my lying down; you are familiar with all my ways. Before a word is on my tongue you know it completely, O LORD. You hem me in—behind and before; you have laid your hand upon me. Such knowledge is too wonderful for me, too lofty for me to attain (Psalm 139:1-6).

Perhaps David began realizing this when God chose him to be king. He had several older brothers, and each one seemed more qualified for the job. When the prophet Samuel paid a visit to David's family, David wasn't even invited to the meeting.

David was a simple shepherd who spent a lot of time alone with his sheep. He may have wondered, "Does anyone really know me?" Yet Someone was always with him. God knew David's heart, and that was the most important qualification for becoming king.

You too may wonder if anyone really knows you. If so, you can be sure that God knows not only how many hairs are on your head but also how many cares are in your heart. He knows everything you do, all that you long for, and every part of who you are. You are lovingly, intimately known.

Sometimes that knowledge scares us. We imagine

that God must be shaking an angry finger at us or sighing with disappointment if He truly knows every thought we have and every word we speak. But that's the beautiful gift of grace. When we come to Christ, His sacrifice enables our complete acceptance. Yes, God continues to bring about changes in our lives. But we truly are free from condemnation.

We all long to be fully known—and loved anyway. God placed that desire in us, and only He can fulfill it. He invites us to far more than a place where everybody knows our names. Instead, He offers a true home for our hearts where we're always welcome, deeply loved, and known completely.

You are known.

Reflect

Read 1 Samuel 16:1-13. How do you feel when you are with someone who knows you well?

Do you have any fears about God knowing you completely? What are they?

What is the truth your heart needs to hear from Him?

Respond

Lord, I'm so glad You know me completely and love me fully. I especially want to say…

Sometimes it seems we live almost invisibly…
laundry, kids, work, groceries.
Does anyone notice?
Does anyone really know us?
Yes, sweet girl, yes.
There is One who watches you.
He sees that extra patience when you're tired.
He sees that smile you give
even when you've got none left.
He sees that last dish you wash,
that first-thing-in-the-morning
report you finish.
You matter to Him.
You and all you do.
He numbers the hairs on your head.
He counts the cares in your heart.
He knows you.
He notices you.
And He loves what He sees.
You may not feel appreciated at times,
but the heart of heaven applauds you.
Well done, daughter of His, *well done.*

FIFTEEN

Strong

I can do everything through him
who gives me strength.

PHILIPPIANS 4:13

Since 1941, the superheroine Wonder Woman has captured our imaginations. She uses her beauty, strength, and superpowers to bring justice to the world. William Moulton Marston created Wonder Woman to represent all that women could be in a time when they did not have much power or influence in society. Rather than relying on brute force, Wonder Woman used love and her lasso of truth to get things done.

Today women sometimes joke about feeling as if we need to be like Wonder Woman in our daily lives. We often juggle a career, kids, marriage, friendships, and church activities. We start the day exhausted and end it the same way. Yet we push ahead, feeling sure we too are called to be superheroines who save the world. We pay the price with our bodies, hearts, and minds.

Many of us also harbor a secret—one we share with only a few people. Despite our Herculean efforts, our endless giving, and our selfless devotion...*they never feel like enough.* There is always another load of laundry to do, another hurting heart to comfort, another Bible study to attend. We silently wonder, "If this is the abundant life, why am I so *tired*?"

I'll admit that I've often struggled with this question. As a type A, motivated, goal-oriented woman, I can wear myself out in a hurry. Wonder Woman and I are a bit different. She knows her mission, and that's all she does. She also knows both her powers and her limitations. I, on the other hand, look at Philippians 4:13 and say, "I can do everything...so that's what I'd better do." But I'm learning that God never calls me to do it all. My mission isn't to save the world; Jesus has already done that. My mission also isn't to be like my neighbors or the women I admire in my Bible study.

In *The Path: Creating Your Mission Statement for Work and Life*, author Laurie Beth Jones says, "You are either living your mission or you are living someone else's."[13] Wonder Woman would be in trouble if she tried to be Superman, and vice versa. Yet we often try to step outside of who God created us to be and operate outside of the power He has given us. The two most important words in Philippians 4:13 are "through him." When we are connected to God, we can do what He has called us to do and be who He has called us to be.

The world tells us we need to do it all; Jesus reminds

us that we're called to fulfill a unique purpose. We can recognize our God-given strengths and respect our limitations. And when we do, the power we have through Christ exceeds anything we can imagine. In the kingdom of God, we're all Wonder Women.

You are strong.

Reflect

Read Philippians 4:4-13. What is God asking you to focus on during this time of your life?

How do the strengths He's given you help in those areas?

Is there anything God might be asking you to say yes or no to right now?

Respond

Lord, thank You for the strength that is mine through You. I want to use that strength to do Your will today, especially in this situation or relationship:

Life is hard sometimes—
crazy, mixed-up, messed up.
And there you are in the middle of it all,
just doing your thing...
being strong and brave
and beautiful
like it's no big deal.
But let me tell you, girl,
it is.
Not everyone can do what you can do.
Not everyone can handle
things the way you can.
And while you wonder sometimes
if you're doing okay...
the rest of us are just
watching in wonder.

SIXTEEN

Beautiful

My lover spoke and said to me, "Arise, my
darling, my beautiful one, and come with me."

SONG OF SOLOMON 2:10

Just flip through a few television channels, and it's easy to see that our culture is obsessed with beauty. Stars get plastic surgery before they walk the red carpet. Makeover shows transform lives and faces. The Miss America pageant crowns one girl the fairest of them all. From the time we are young girls, we wonder how we fit into all of this fuss about beauty.

I clearly remember changing outfits at least a dozen times the evening before the first day of sixth grade. I would put one on, parade in front of my parents, and then rush back to my room to stare in the mirror. None of them seemed quite right. I was a wallflower who got few compliments. The next morning I woke up to find a note beside my bed. It said, "The outfit looks great, and so do you. Love, Dad." I don't think he even knew which outfit I ended up choosing. It didn't matter. I belonged to him, and that made me beautiful in his eyes no matter what I was wearing.

Our heavenly Father feels the same way about us. He created us, and regardless of what the world may try to tell us, He thinks we're beautiful. I attended a conference taught by my dear friend, fellow writer, and women's ministry leader Bekah Mulvaney. She talked about women's search for acceptance and how she is learning to embrace God's view of her. She said, "When I look in the mirror I see my imperfections. When God looks at me He probably thinks I'm adorable! After all, He made this nose, these eyes, and my heart."

You may think, "But I have so much ugliness and sin on the inside." But if you belong to Christ, you have been forgiven. When you come to know Him, you become a new creation. We are the bride of Christ, and His sacrifice on the cross transforms all that's unlovely within us. Yes, He still works in our lives to conform us to His image. But He looks at us with love and grace. As the old saying goes, beauty is in the eye of the beholder.

The Song of Solomon is thought by many scholars to be a picture of Christ and His relationship with us. Over and over the lover tells his beloved, "You are beautiful."

In *Do You Think I'm Beautiful? The Question Every Woman Asks*, Angela Thomas shares how we can respond to our desire for beauty.

If the question, "Do you think I'm beautiful?" came attached to my soul, then maybe the answer wasn't ever meant to fully come from this world. Maybe the purpose of the question is to take me by the hand and walk me into the presence of the Creator. My soul cries out and asks me the questions meant to lead me to God. Maybe all that really matters is what He thinks of me.[14]

Whether we obsess about it or ignore it, we're made to know we're beautiful. That truth can ultimately come only from God. He's waiting to speak to our hearts the words we've always longed to hear.

You are beautiful.

Reflect

Read Song of Solomon 2:1-13. What were you taught about beauty (inside and outside) as a young girl?

How did that shape your view of yourself?

Do you believe God thinks you're beautiful? Why or why not?

Respond

Lord, the world has told me so many lies about beauty that it's hard to know the truth. I pray You will show me how You see me, both inside and out. I praise You for creating me, and I want to say…

You started in God's heart,
were shaped by His hands
and presented to the world as a *gift*.
No matter how it feels,
no matter what you've been through,
that's still true.
You are of great worth,
the only YOU ever made.
There's a part of *who God is*
that gets expressed only through who you are.
You're a bearer of His image.
And that's *beautiful.*
It's beautiful in a way that's deeper
and truer than the latest trend.
It's a forever kind of beauty that time
can't touch or years take away.
God sees it in you
and because you believe it, make it yours…
we see Him in you too.

SEVENTEEN

Delightful

The LORD delights in those who fear him,
who put their hope in his unfailing love.

PSALM 147:11

I frequently ask my counseling clients a simple question: What brings you joy? Answers I often receive include "Spending time with family," "Being with my favorite pet," or "Having coffee with friends." As these women share with me, a shift inevitably occurs. Light comes to their eyes, and smiles cross their faces. Their voices get clearer and stronger. Delight, which is a synonym for joy, is powerful.

If you asked God the same question, what do you think He would say? As amazing as it may sound, one of His answers would be "You." The Bible tells us in several places that the Lord delights in His people. As I looked up these verses, I kept scratching my head. "Surely not. I know God loves me. He forgives me. But delight? That's a bit much." Yet over and over the answer is clear. I'm a delight to God. And so are you.

This inspired me to dig a little deeper. Why does

God delight in us, as imperfect as we are? The answer is simple and yet profound. When we receive Christ as our Savior, we truly are in right relationship with God. "Love covers over a multitude of sins" (1 Peter 4:8). Imagine a little girl's first trip to the zoo with her parents, complete with a few dozen giggles, a hundred pictures, and a thousand smiles. It's pure delight on both sides.

Now imagine you walked up to the parents and said, "Your daughter threw a fit in front of the monkey cage. She spilled her drink in the cafeteria. And she begged for a toy she didn't need in the gift shop. How can you delight in her?" You would most likely get quizzical looks from her parents as if they didn't even understand how you could ask such a question. Love is able to delight even if it also sometimes has to discipline.

It's reassuring to know God can delight in us now, just as we are, and that He will do the same forever in heaven when we truly are made perfect. That brings up a second question: What about us brings God delight? Looking back to Psalm 147:11, we see two phrases that show us the answer. God delights in those who fear Him and those who hope in His unfailing love. Like the little girl at the zoo with her parents, true delight is all about *relationship*. God delights in our love for Him, our obedience, and our desire to know Him.

Most of us are familiar with Psalm 37:4—"Delight yourself in the Lord and he will give you the desires of your heart." It's a beautiful, endless cycle. We delight in God, and He delights in us. This picture is very different from the somber and serious one we often see on Sunday morning. Our relationship with God is intended to be filled with joy and mutual satisfaction. Merriam Webster's dictionary actually defines *delight* as "something that gives great pleasure."

It seems scandalous, doesn't it? Even as I write these words I feel a bit of fear and trembling. The God of the universe just seems too big, too awesome to delight in me. Yet He is also a God who desires a relationship with us. When we love Him deeply, seek Him persistently, and follow Him faithfully, we make the heart of God smile.

You are delightful.

Reflect

Read Psalm 147. What brings you joy?

How does knowing that God delights in you make you feel?

What's one way you can make His heart smile today?

Respond

Lord, I'm awed and amazed that I am a delight to You. You are a delight to my heart too. You have brought me so much joy by…

and I want to bring You joy by…

⌒

Psst…
Come close and I'll tell you a secret.
Will you dare to believe it's true?
God delights in *you*.
When you love Him,
believe what He says,
choose to truly be who He made you,
you bring *joy* to His heart.
Can you sense the smile of heaven today?
It's coming your way.

EIGHTEEN

Creative

In the beginning God created.
GENESIS 1:1

The first time we catch a glimpse of God, we see an artist sculpting the world with His words. In seven days a masterpiece is finished. Then God declares, "It is very good." We are part of that creation, made in His image—and because of that, part of us is inherently creative as well.

You may be shaking your head. "Not me. I'm not creative." We often define creativity too narrowly. We think of it in terms of words on a page or paint on a canvas. But creativity is essentially bringing something into existence that wasn't there before. God is the ultimate Creator because only He can make something out of nothing. But He allows each of us to share in a little of His creativity as well. Whitney Hopler explores this truth in *A Creative Life: God's Design for You.*

> The secular view of creativity portrays this God-given gift as a special talent reserved only for

people who are artistic, or for children who can afford to have fun before they're shackled by the practical demands of life as adults. But God, the master Creator and source of all creativity, has a far more holistic view. He has created you in His image, and will enable you to participate in His creativity. He wants you to live creatively at all times and in all situations, so your life can become the masterpiece He intends it to be.[15]

Your version of creativity may show up in the kitchen when you make delicious meals. It might be revealed in the way you decorate your house. Or it could find expression in your ability to talk to anyone. When God made you, He built creativity into your DNA in some way.

We tend to think of God the Father as the Creator, but John tells us that Christ had an essential role. "He was with God in the beginning. Through him all things were made; without him nothing was made that has been made" (John 1:2-3). Christ is the key to our creativity. When we give our lives to Him, "we have the mind of Christ" (1 Corinthians 2:16). That means we have access to endless innovation and creativity. The God who made the world lives within us. Just as He often shows His love through us, He also shows His creativity.

The world has tried to tell us that creativity belongs to certain people or professions. But God makes it clear that true creativity belongs to Him. He chooses to display it through each of us in ways that are surprising, unique, and endless. We are His pages, canvases, and melodies.

In the beginning God created…and He still does through you.

You are creative.

Reflect

Read Genesis 1. Complete this sentence: Creativity is…

Do you usually see yourself as a creative person? Why or why not?

Describe one way God might show His creativity through you.

Respond

Lord, You are the Creator of everything, and You live within me. Please help me display Your creativity in the unique ways You intended when You made me. Thank You for giving me the ability to…

You are paint on God's canvas.
Notes in His song.
Words on His page.
Created *by* Him
and then blessed to create *with* Him.
In your everyday life,
your work, your relationships,
you bring Him to the world in new ways.
And when you do,
it is so again…
"God saw all that he had made
and it was very good."

NINETEEN

His Friend

*I no longer call you servants, because a servant does
not know his master's business. Instead, I have
called you friends, for everything that I learned
from my Father I have made known to you.*

JOHN 15:15

Lord Knutsford and Lord Cross shared a friendship
that lasted several decades, and the two died only
three weeks apart. In 1914 the *New York Times*
stated, "Their athletic, professional, political, and social
friendship lasted nearly seventy years, a remarkable
record."[16] In more recent times, two California women
named Annabelle and Shirley have outlasted even this
impressive length. Annabelle, age 89, says, "We have
shared happy and sad times, trials and tribulations and
have always been there for each other."[17]

We all long for a friendship that will last a lifetime,
yet it's often difficult to find. A recent poll found that
"Americans have a third fewer close friends and confi-
dantes than just two decades ago—a sign that people
may be living lonelier, more isolated lives than in the

past."[18] Moves, disagreements, and the busyness of life often draw people apart over time. Yet we do have a friend who has promised to be there for us always. It's not our neighbor, the woman we met at Bible study last week, or even our college roommate. This friend is one we'd never expect.

We're human. He's divine.

We're fallen. He's perfect.

We're broken. He's complete.

Yet Jesus says to each of us when we give our hearts to Him, "You are not just My servant—you are My friend." When you hear that, perhaps you (like me) tend to think, "Well, maybe I could be God's friend, but He probably doesn't really like me. He just tolerates me." Ask Annabelle and Shirley if tolerating someone is the same as friendship. Sure, through the years, they have probably frustrated and disappointed each other. But that is far outweighed by all the true characteristics of friendship—joy, delight, connection, warmth, belonging, grace, support, and companionship. Friendship is about sharing life together, the ups and downs, victories and defeats, laughter and tears.

Friendship is a safe haven for our hearts. It's the place where we can most authentically be ourselves and lay before another person all that we are without fear. You may have been hurt by others. Perhaps a friend has betrayed you, let you down, or simply disappeared from your life when you needed her most. You may not even know what having a real friend is like. And yet a quiet longing within you continues to ask, like a child on the playground, "Will you be my friend?" To that question Jesus replies with a resounding yes! He backed up His commitment by going to the cross. "Greater love has no one than this, that he lay down his life for his friends" (John 15:13).

Perhaps many years from now someone will ask you the question someone asked Annabelle and Shirley: "Do you have a friendship that has lasted a lifetime?" You'll be able to answer with your whole heart, "Yes, and it will last for all eternity."

You are God's friend.

Reflect

Read John 15:9-17. What does the word *friend* mean to you?

Is it difficult for you to see yourself as God's friend? Why or why not?

Looking back over your life, what are some ways God has been a friend to you?

Respond

Lord, I'm so grateful You are not only the God of
the universe but also my friend. Thank You for
being a great friend to me by…

As children we ask,
"Will you be my friend?"
And as the years go by,
that question never really goes away.
We just speak it with our
hearts rather than our lips.
Listen to the answer from
One Who Loves You…
"Yes, I will be your friend.
I'll stick by you in happy and hard times.
I'll cheer you on, hold you up,
and always love you enough to say what's true.
Friends for life,
friends forever…
that's Me and you."

TWENTY

His Messenger

*Go into all the world and preach
the good news to all creation.*

MARK 16:15

Today when we hear the word *messenger*, the first thing that may come to mind is the software created by Microsoft. But long before Bill Gates came along, messengers had a much different role in society. Instead of e-mail or even snail mail, long-distance communication in the ancient world usually consisted of one person hand-carrying a written letter to another. If you were someone very wealthy, such as a king, you had messengers to do that work for you.

Being a messenger in ancient times might appear to have been an easy job, but it actually had a long list of requirements. First, trustworthiness was a must. The letters sent often contained important information that had to be handled with the utmost care and discretion. A messenger also had to be loyal. The king needed to be sure that his words would not somehow land in the hands of his enemies. Finally, those who carried the letters of the king needed to be good representatives of him. In the times before television and the Internet, most people never directly saw or heard the one sending the message. The messenger stood in his place.

Being a messenger was an honor and a privilege. When the king chose someone to carry his words, he was saying, "I trust you not only to do what I have asked but also to be a reflection of who I am." When God calls us to be His messengers, He is saying the same. Until we are in heaven, no one will see Him face-to-face. So instead, we are called to be His hands, His feet, His heart, and His mouth.

There's a legend about a European town that had a statue of Jesus. During the World War II bombings, the statue was damaged. Miraculously, every part remained intact except the hands. The townspeople responded by posting a sign that said, "Now we're the only hands Jesus has." Regardless of whether the account is historically true, the truth in its message resonates with our hearts. When Christ returned to His Father in heaven, the disciples could have posted a similar sign: "Now we're the only messengers Jesus has."

You may wonder how this could be. "Me, a messenger? My life seems so ordinary." Ordinariness has never been an obstacle to God. Consider David the shepherd. Mary the small-town girl. Peter the fisherman. The messenger may be ordinary, but the message is *extraordinary*.

The apostle Paul says, "We have this treasure in jars of clay to show that this all-surpassing power is from God and not from us" (2 Corinthians 4:7).

The way you share the message will be as unique as you are. You don't have to be a writer or preacher to share the good news. You may be God's messenger by living with integrity in your workplace, by raising godly children, or by the kindness you show to your neighbors. God has wired you to share His message in distinctive, wonderful ways that reflect His heart and His design for you.

The God of the universe has chosen *you* to be His messenger. He picked you to represent Him. By doing so, He declares to all the world, "Yes, she belongs to me!"

You are God's messenger.

Reflect

Read Mark 16:9-20. How does it make you feel to know God has chosen you to represent Him?

What message does He want you to share with others?

How can you express that message through who you are and what you do today?

Respond

Lord, I feel honored and humbled when I think
about how You have chosen me to be Your messenger. Show me how I can do that today. I want
to help others know the truth that…

You've got a message to bring to the world.
With everything you do, you show it.
With everything you are, you share it.
Your life is a declaration
written by the heart of God,
and He sees you as worthy to go on His behalf.
You are chosen, sent, entrusted with the Word.
You're an ambassador of grace,
a carrier of hope,
a bringer of blessings wherever you are.
So go out there with heart and head held high
as one who is highly favored by the King!

TWENTY-ONE

Heard

You heard my cry for mercy when
I called to you for help.

PSALM 31:22

The ice storm swept in while I slept, blanketing the backyard in white and consigning my car to the driveway. My husband was out of town on a business trip. "We'll be okay," I assured the dog as she looked up at me from a pile of blankets. The day wore on, and sleet pounded against the roof like an unwelcome visitor. I spent the following night without heat or electricity in a sleeping bag we had bought in Colorado. Back then, I thought its low-temperature rating seemed a bit excessive. But now as I curled up in it, I was thankful for every bit of insulation.

The next day brought more of the same, and as the house grew colder, my sense of fear grew stronger. When I saw that my cell phone died, my heart skipped a beat. Until then, waiting out the storm had felt like an adventure. But being cut off from the outside world made me suddenly realize the danger. I sat down on the edge of the bed and prayed. "Lord, I know You're going to take care of me, but I'm scared. What should I do?"

At that very moment I heard a knock on the door. Concerned that her calls had gone unanswered, my dear friend Cynthia had sent her husband, Brian, to check on me. He offered to take my dog and me to their house until our power returned. With great relief, I accepted. I spent the next two days safe and warm. I shiver when I think of what those two days could have been like if someone hadn't come to rescue me.

As I considered the timing, I realized that God had answered my prayer even before I spoke it. God had put me on Cynthia's heart that morning. Two other friends had also sounded the alarm when I couldn't be reached. Brian was already on his way to get me when I spoke my words of fear and desperation. God not only heard my prayer but also saw my situation and knew my need even before I put it into words.

Our prayers aren't always answered this way. Sometimes God waits long past the time when we think we should be rescued. When Lazarus became sick, Jesus waited three more days to go see him. By the time He arrived, Lazarus was gone. Martha, the sister of Lazarus, protested and said, "If you had been here, my brother would not have died" (John 11:21). Yet Jesus revealed when He raised Lazarus from the dead that He had already been listening and answering—just not in the way Mary or Martha expected. We live in a fallen world, so some answers may not come this side of heaven. But God promises that one day we will understand.

In our everyday lives, we wait and pray for lots of things—positive job interviews, good test results, mended relationships, or other breakthroughs. And even when we seem to hear nothing at all—when the house is getting colder and the danger is increasing—we can be sure God knows and cares. Silence isn't the absence of God hearing, but rather the sound of Him listening.

You are heard.

Reflect

Read Psalm 31. Describe a time when God answered a prayer in your life.

What question or request are you waiting for Him to answer now?

What helps you have hope while you're waiting for His answer?

Respond

Lord, I praise You for loving me and hearing my
prayers. Help me to be patient and trust You for…

⸺

Sometimes it seems
as if silence is heaven's only answer.
But lean close enough into that silence
and you'll hear a heartbeat within it.
Love…love…love…
This rhythm isn't always a yes to what we want
or what we may think we need
but it's a YES
to His ways, His plans,
so much higher than ours.
And YES
to who we are,
to our relationship with Him,
to what's forever best.
You are heard.
You are loved.
You are held close in the arms
of One who listens,
even in the silence,
to every word.

TWENTY-TWO

Carried

I have made you and I will carry you.

Isaiah 46:4

The plane takes off as we giggle nervously. With room for only eight passengers, this is hardly a luxury flight. There are no stewardesses offering peanuts as my family and I soar over pristine waters and the vibrant green trees of the Alaskan wilderness. We see places we could never go on our own. After a wonderful flight, the pilot says, "I hope you enjoyed the ride."

Later I think about the places I feel called to go in life—not spots on a map, but destinations God has written onto my heart. Sometimes they feel as tall as those Alaskan peaks, and I wonder how I'll ever reach them.

But then God shows up and says, "Get on board, girl." I step inside His will and take a seat, and soon we're moving. I'm learning our job isn't to fly. Oh, I still try it sometimes. I flap my arms until I'm exhausted and then wonder why my feet are still on the ground. Our job is obedience—to get on the plane, to let God carry us.

Being carried doesn't mean being passive. It means

being in a dependent relationship. We take action, but we leave the ultimate responsibility and results to God, determine the destination.

Sometimes that's scary. As I looked out the window on that plane in Alaska, the mountains were a little too close for comfort. But the pilot kept us safe, and he let us see and experience things we never imagined. When we landed, we felt exhilarated.

When God calls us to go somewhere in life, He also promises to get us there. When we trust, yield, and let Him carry us, everything changes. And that baggage you've brought with you? He'll carry that too. Just step on board, settle in, lean back, and let love take you higher than you ever thought you could go.

You are carried.

Reflect

Read Isaiah 46:3-10. What burdens are you carrying?

How can you let God carry them (and you) instead?

Describe a time in your life when God took you to a new place with Him.

Respond

Lord, thank You that I don't have to strive. It's amazing to know You will carry me. Help me to rest in Your love and trust You to get me where You want me to go. Please carry me through…

I rest my head on the pillow
without much rest in my heart.
To-dos swirl around in my mind.
Tasks fall heavy on my shoulders.
I silently pray,
"Lord, give me the grace
to carry all of this."
It seems I hear a whisper in response,
"Ask instead for the grace
to let Me carry you."
I once saw a little girl carrying a rock too big,
determined to take it home.
Sweat beading, little feet laboring.
Then Daddy came and swooped her up.
Joy. Giggles. Grace.
She still held the rock, but it no longer
weighed her down, because someone held her.
I fall asleep with a smile…
thoughts as light as love.

TWENTY-THREE

His Light

You are the light of the world.

MATTHEW 5:14

The news headlines drifted in from the living room as I sat at my desk. The story of yet another tragedy contrasted so sharply with what I was writing that I stopped, sighed, and leaned back in my chair. A sense of despair washed over me. "Lord," I silently prayed, "is there *anything* I can do about the darkness in this world? It seems so overwhelming." I sensed a gentle whisper within my heart replying, "The only way to get rid of the darkness is to add more light."

Darkness is the absence of light. Trying to go after it directly is like chasing your shadow. You can't bag it up and throw it away. Only light is powerful enough to make the darkness disappear. During the Sermon on the Mount, Jesus made it clear that we are the light of the world. We are called to shine. But the light we share is not our own.

From the very beginning of creation, God has been the source of light both spiritually and literally.

Genesis 1:2-3 says, "Darkness was over the surface of the deep, and the Spirit of God was hovering over the waters. And God said, 'Let there be light,' and there was light." Imagine a world full of darkness. Then with four small words, light blazes forth. Every living thing in our world relies on light for its existence—plants, animals, and people. The God who brought light to the world also brings it to our lives. As 2 Corinthians 4:6 says, "For God, who said, 'Let light shine out of darkness,' made his light shine in our hearts."

The best part of all is that we don't have to be like the lightbulb that said, "I have to find a way to shine!" The lightbulb went to a conference to learn about its inner capacity for light. It read books about how to brighten someone's day. Each morning the lightbulb would get up and recite positive affirmations. "I am a lightbulb. I believe in myself. I will shine!" But nothing happened. Eventually the lightbulb became weary and discouraged. It began to doubt who it was and what it could do. It almost burned out completely. Fortunately, one day the lightbulb was carefully placed in a fixture. Light burst forth from it and filled the room. The lightbulb finally understood that the key was not to try harder, but to plug into the source.

Trying to shine on our own can be exhausting. Instead, we are simply called to be closely connected to God and remain in Him. When we do, His light pours forth through us in powerful, brilliant ways that change the world. The ways we shine may not make the news, but they make a difference.

You are the light of the world.

Reflect

Read Matthew 5:14-20. Do you tend to plug into God, try to shine on your own, or both?

How can you tell the difference?

What's one simple way you can bring light into someone's life today?

Respond

Lord, I believe You are the source of all light and You live within me. Help me stay connected to You so I can shine wherever I go. I ask for Your help to...

You glow
with His love
in ways that make
a difference in this world.
And you do more than
light up a room—
you light up the hearts
of all who are in it.
So stand tall,
daughter of His,
share the joy,
and shine on.

TWENTY-FOUR

Defended

The LORD will fight for you; you need only to be still.

EXODUS 14:14

In 1966, Rubin "Hurricane" Carter was arrested for three murders he didn't commit, and in 1967, he was convicted. The highly acclaimed middleweight boxer spent the next two decades in jail despite his innocence. This forceful man who had once been able to defend himself against anyone now found himself powerless and alone. While in prison, Rubin shared his story in his bestselling autobiography, *The Sixteenth Round*.

Through the book, a young man named Lesra Martin learned of Rubin's situation. A father-son relationship developed between them, and Lesra became determined to bring Rubin home. With the help of friends, Lesra came to Rubin's defense when everyone else had given up. The compelling movie *The Hurricane* shares Rubin's fight for freedom. He eventually learned what many of us take a lifetime to discover—love is the most powerful defense of all.

We all feel a bit like Rubin at times, weighed down by unjust accusations, hurtful words, and misplaced blame. Our first instinct is to react like a boxer in a ring. Throw a punch. Dodge and weave. Make sure our opponent goes down so we can't be attacked again. But as Rubin discovered, that kind of response only goes so far and often hurts those we love.

Fortunately, we do have Someone who promises to come to our defense. God says He will defend us and fight for us when we have been wronged. As Lesra Martin befriended Rubin Carter, our Advocate comes to us just when it seems we should give up. He will stop at nothing to make sure we are freed. His truth is more powerful than any accusation. Most of all, He uses love to fight the battle. Sometimes we think of love as being wimpy or soft. But love can also be relentless and fierce.

God doesn't simply fight for what we want. Sometimes things may not even turn out the way we'd like. But He is always willing to fight for what we need. He will stop at nothing to free us from bitterness, protect us from despair, and lift us from shame.

Also, God isn't usually fighting against other people. It's easy to point our finger at "them" and assume "they" are the enemy. But "our struggle is not against flesh and blood, but against the rulers, against the authorities, against the powers of this dark world and against the spiritual forces of evil in the heavenly realms" (Ephesians 6:12).

While Lesra and his friends worked around the clock, Rubin remained in his cell. It seemed he could do little. Sometimes we are called to be still while God fights for us (Exodus 14:14). God often calls us to be part of the battle, but the most difficult command can be to wait and let Him bring us deliverance. Yet if we join in when He hasn't called us to, we risk being wounded even more than before.

There are also times when the battle may not be won in this world. God doesn't promise us justice now, but He does promise it in eternity. In the meantime, you can be certain He is fighting for you and will continue to until all is made right forever.

Toward the end of the movie, Rubin makes a powerful statement when Lesra comes to visit him. He says, "Hate put me in here; love is going to bust me out." With God as our Defender, we can all say the same.

You are defended.

Reflect

Read Exodus 14:14-31. What does it mean to you to have God as your Defender?

Describe a time when you felt He protected or defended you.

What battle do you need to trust Him with now?

Respond

Lord, I praise You for being my Defender. I'm so glad I can trust You completely with my life. I especially need You to…

⌐

You have a Defender
who knows your name,
who fights on your behalf
who protects your heart.
He surrounds you with love,
fortifies you with favor,
keeps you in His care.
The battles rage,
and yes, in this fallen world,
sometimes we are wounded.
But with Him on our side
we can be sure
we will never be defeated.

TWENTY-FIVE

Guided

*I will instruct you and teach you in the way you
should go; I will counsel you and watch over you.*

PSALM 32:8

M y car came with a GPS. It includes a small
screen with a map and a bossy woman who
tells me what to do and where to go. She and
I have a somewhat challenging relationship. She often
sternly says to me, "Make a U-turn." If I'd designed the
system, she would say, "You've had a hard day. Isn't that
an ice cream store down the road?"

In spite of her unsympathetic manner, I do appreciate her directions. She helps me find restaurants, gas
stations, and other necessary stops. She tells me exactly
where I am and where I'm going. I've discovered that
the secret to making the system work is to listen. Sometimes I drive along talking, listening to the radio, or just
daydreaming, I vaguely hear her say, "Turn right in 500
feet," but I zip right by (hence the U-turns).

I tend to do the same in my relationship with God.
I pray about a situation and ask Him, "Where do I go?

What do I do?" Then I get so busy with life that when He responds, I don't hear His instructions. Then I wonder why I end up somewhere I never wanted to be.

There are certain phrases God speaks to my heart that I do hear. One of those is, "If you're driven, you can't be led." I tend to move forward at warp speed, do ten things at once, and exhaust myself in the process. Then I struggle to follow God because I'm so far down the wrong road.

It's immensely comforting to know that He has promised to guide me if only I'll let Him. When the Israelites went to the Promised Land, God's presence traveled with them in the form of a cloud. "Whether the cloud stayed over the tabernacle for two days or a month or a year, the Israelites would remain in camp and not set out; but when it lifted, they would set out. At the LORD's command they encamped, and at the LORD's command they set out" (Numbers 9:22-23). God was the Israelites' divine GPS system then, and He is still ours today.

DaySpring cofounder Roy Lessin wrote, "Sometimes we can be led to think that God's work is dependent upon us, upon what we do, and upon what we know. The truth is that God wants us to be totally dependent upon Him." Roy added this poem:

> God is not looking for those who are clever,
> but for those in whom He can be wise;

He is not looking for those who are talented,
but for those to whom He can be all-sufficient;
He is not looking for those who are powerful,
but for those through whom He can be almighty.[19]

I would add that God is not looking for those who are getting ahead, but for those He can lead.

If you're wondering which way to go today, pause and listen for a still, small voice. You might hear it immediately or later. It could come through a Scripture you read, a trusted friend, or another way you never expected. You don't have to figure everything out for yourself because you have a divine GPS (God Positioning System). He'll always get you where you need to go.

You are guided.

Reflect

Read Psalm 32:6-11. Do you naturally tend to be driven or to be led? Why?

In what situation or area of your life do you need God to give you direction today?

Describe a time God guided you in the past.

Respond

Lord, I'm so glad You will lead me. I commit to
follow You. I ask for Your guidance about…

———

Here's the thing…
it's hard to redirect someone
who is standing still.
Yes, there are seasons for staying.
This is about the seasons of going, setting out,
those times when your heart is restless
and your feet are ready.
If that's you, then go without fear.
God is with you, for you, behind you,
and ahead of you.
And even if you lose your way for a bit,
even if you grow weary,
even if you don't know which
direction to go at times,
His purposes will prevail.
Take that step, woman of courage,
and know that love goes with you all the way.

TWENTY-SIX

His Child

*How great is the love the Father has lavished
on us, that we should be called children
of God! And that is what we are!*

1 JOHN 3:1

She sat in my counseling office with her eyes lowered, silently reading the paper in her hand. It listed all the ways God loved her. She paused, shook her head, and pointed, "I don't know if I can believe this one about God being my loving heavenly Father. My earthly father abused me, and I just can't help seeing God the same way. I'm afraid of what He'll do to me." I wish I could say this scene was never repeated, but it is, over and over again. In a variety of ways, with many different words, women walk through my door and tell me that the one man who was supposed to love and protect them chose to abuse or abandon them instead.

Yet within each woman there still lives a dream of the father she's longed for all her life. One woman in her fifties confides how she hopes for a close relationship with her dad even though he's in his eighties and still treats her harshly. Another woman speaks wistfully of a father long gone and wonders how life would have been different if he had chosen his family instead of a bottle. Even those with good relationships with their dads can point to a word that wounded or a habit that harmed.

If that's the case, why do we keep striving to fill that void? I believe it's because that place in our hearts was never intended to be filled by an earthly father. Instead, it's meant to create an ache within us that can be filled only by our heavenly Father. Just as women are drawn to love stories because we are the bride of Christ, we are also in pursuit of the ultimate dad because we are the daughters of God.

In *Abba's Child: The Cry of the Heart for Intimate Belonging*, Brennan Manning explains that when he sensed God's fatherly feelings toward him, his life was transformed. "Let us pause here. It is God who has called us by name. The God beside whose beauty the Grand Canyon is only a shadow has called us beloved. The God beside whose power the nuclear bomb is nothing has tender feelings for us."[20] Your true Father, the Daddy your heart has longed for all your life, is the God of the universe.

If your heart skipped a beat and you were tempted to put down the book after reading that last line, then there's a lie in your heart you still believe. Maybe your dad valued rules over relationship, so you imagine God as a divine taskmaster. Perhaps your dad left early in your life and never reappeared, so you see God as distant. Even worse, your dad may have abused you in ways that left physical or emotional scars that you'll bear the rest of your life, so you see God as unpredictable and unsafe.

But your heavenly Father wants to replace those lies with the truth. He has promised never to abuse you and to instead be your Protector (Psalm 18:2). He has promised never to abandon you and instead to be with you always (Matthew 28:20). He has promised to accept you as you are and love you more than you can imagine (Ephesians 3:17-19). The dream in your heart for the perfect dad never leaves because God has always intended to make it come true. The father you've always wanted is the Father you already have.

You are His child.

Reflect

Read 1 John 3:1-10. How has your earthly father influenced your view of God?

Are there any lies you believe about your heavenly Father as a result? What's the truth?

What have you longed for in your relationship with your dad that you need God to give you?

Respond

Lord, I realize that only You can fill the void inside me that longs for a perfect father-daughter relationship. I thank You for being my heavenly Father, and as Your child I ask You to...

Sweet child,
You are loved by your Father.
The dream of you began in His heart,
and He welcomed you into the world with joy.
He knit you together in your mother's womb
and knew all your days before
one of them came to be.
Even if others hurt, abandon, or betray you...
your heavenly Daddy is with you, for you,
and He'll never leave.
He looks at you with love and says,
"She's mine."

TWENTY-SEVEN

Understood

*The heart is deceitful above all things and
beyond cure. Who can understand it? "I the
LORD search the heart and examine the mind."*

JEREMIAH 17:9-10

In the telephone game, one person whispers a sentence into another's ear, who whispers it to another, and on down the line. The last person says aloud what she thinks she heard, which is often wildly inaccurate. "Susie has a dog named Spot" can quickly turn into "Susie likes Matt a lot."

Most of us stopped playing the telephone game long ago, but we still know what it means to be misunderstood. We tell a friend we like her hair short, and she hears, "I don't like your hair long." We ask our husband for help with the dishes, and he thinks we're saying, "You're not helping enough around the house." We shake our heads and wonder how an innocent comment can erupt into a disagreement so quickly.

So we head to the self-help section to learn how to fix the problem. Books tell us that if we can just learn to understand ourselves, everyone else will follow suit. But the closer we look inside, the more we discover we're a mystery as well. We want to lose weight, but we eat too many cookies. We long to be kind to our kids, but we raise our voices. We desire to follow God faithfully but find ourselves wandering off the path. We don't seem to understand ourselves very well either.

This dilemma is nothing new. The prophet Jeremiah wondered long ago, "The heart is deceitful above all things and beyond cure. Who can understand it?" Fortunately, God stepped in and answered the question by saying, "I the LORD search the heart and examine the mind." There is Someone who understands you completely. All of your motives, mysteries, and misunderstandings are clear to Him. He knows what you do and why you do it. The best psychologist in the world can't hold a candle to the light God can shed on your heart and soul. Donna Partow writes about this in *Walking in Total God-Confidence*.

> God is not in the business of keeping secrets. He is not sitting on His heavenly throne with His arms folded, saying, "You gals figure this one out for yourselves." God is always speaking in a myriad of ways: through His Word, through prayer, through other believers, and even through your circumstances.[21]

We grow up learning to pray, "God, help me understand what to do." It seems far more difficult to pray,

"God, help me understand who I am." So we listen to other voices. Every magazine cover at the checkout stand seems to say, "We understand you, and we've got the ten steps to happiness you need." Yet the answers prove to be hollow, and we long again for someone to truly, deeply know every part of us.

In the telephone game, the only way to make sure you've heard correctly is to go back to the source. The same is true when it comes to being understood. When we draw near to the One who knows us completely, we can ask, "What is the truth about who I am? What do You need to show me about my heart?" Whatever the answer may be, you can be sure God's love and grace will come through loud and clear.

You are understood.

Reflect

Read Jeremiah 17:7-14. What messages about who you are go through your mind most often? "I am…"

Are those messages true? If not, what does God say instead? "You are…"

What does it mean to you to be truly loved and understood?

Respond

Lord, I'm so thankful You understand me better than anyone else—even better than I understand myself! I pray You will show me what I need to know about who I am and what I do. I have a question for You today:

God understands hard times.
So when life lets you down,
know that He's holding you up
and will never let you go.
God understands happy times.
So when life brings joy,
know that He's celebrating with you
and sending more blessings your way too.
And the best news of all,
God understands *you*—
what you've been through,
who you are, who you're becoming.
All of life,
all of you.
There's only One who truly gets it…
and He's got you.

TWENTY-EIGHT

Valuable

These [trials] have come so that your faith—
of greater worth than gold, which perishes
even though refined by fire—may be proved
genuine and may result in praise, glory and
honor when Jesus Christ is revealed.

1 PETER 1:7

As I write this, the economy is tumbling. House prices are down, stocks have dropped, and businesses are closing their doors. Yet in the midst of this turmoil, one commodity has retained its value: gold. Until recently, the price of gold even continued to rise. For many years, gold actually backed our currency. Much of it was held in a high-security facility at Fort Knox called the United States Bullion Depository (hence the saying "safer than Fort Knox").

Gold must go through a process before it becomes marketable. It is mined and then refined. All that is not of value must be stripped away so that only the gold remains. But even before that happens, the inherent worth is still there. In gold-mining days, settlers staked out claims based on the slightest glimmer of gold. No one expected to find gold bars sitting on the ground, waiting to be carried off. Speculators understood that gold mining was all about potential.

We are a lot like those gold mines. As long as we are on earth, there will still be some mining and refining to do in our lives. We imagine that we need to be more like Fort Knox—row upon row of glittering gold. But God's economy is different from ours. Yes, He is committed to refining us, but He is more interested in the relationship along the way. God doesn't *need* anything from us. Sometimes we can focus so much on what we need to change, how we should be different, or the impurities that still need to be removed that we forget that God values people more than perfection.

We also sometimes forget the goal of God's refining work in our lives. According to 1 Peter 1:7, our faith is refined to bring praise, glory, and honor to Jesus. It's not even about us—it's about Him. We imagine God shaking His head, sighing, and saying, "Wow, I've got a lot of work to do on her before she can be of any worth to Me." But He is more likely saying, "Wow, look at how much potential she has to bring glory to My Son!"

We are just as precious to God when the refining process begins in our lives as we are when it's completed in heaven. That truth offers our hearts even more security than Fort Knox.

You are valuable.

Reflect

Read 1 Peter 1:3-9. Describe one way God is refining your faith right now.

How are you starting to see more of Him in your life through that process?

What do you think the final result will be?

Respond

Lord, it's so good to know that I am valuable to You right now and that You are refining me even more for Your purposes. I pray You will…

We step on scales.
Compare ourselves to others.
Try to measure up.
We all just want to know,
"What am I worth?"
The Heart of Heaven declares
that the answer is infinite,
beyond our ways,
more than we can know.
Because our worth
doesn't come from
what we do,
but *whom we belong to*.
And you're His treasure…
loved beyond measure.

TWENTY-NINE

Redeemed

*Fear not, for I have redeemed you; I have
summoned you by name; you are mine.*

ISAIAH 43:1

A classic story tells of a boy who worked for months on a little sailboat. He poured his heart into every detail, and the boat became his most valued treasure. One day as the boy played with his beloved creation, a strong current suddenly swept it out of sight. He searched and searched for it, but it seemed to be lost forever. A few weeks later, something familiar caught his eye in the window of a shop. His boat! He ran inside and begged the store owner to return it to him. However, the stern man refused and insisted the boy pay the high price set for the little boat. With tears streaming down his face, the boy returned to the store with all the money he had. He left with a smile on his face and his precious boat in his arms. As he walked back home, he whispered to his creation, "You are twice mine. I made you, and I bought you."

This story resonates with our hearts because it's about

redemption—something we all need. God created us, but we became separated from Him through our sin. Yet He was still willing to pay the ultimate price—the death of His Son—to bring us back home. Even before Christ came, God was seeking the hearts of His people. The word *redeemed* actually appears more in the Old Testament than the New Testament. It has a variety of powerful meanings, as R. David Rightmire explains.

> Finding its context in the social, legal, and religious customs of the ancient world, the metaphor of redemption includes the ideas of loosing from a bond, setting free from captivity or slavery, buying back something lost or sold, exchanging something in one's possession for something possessed by another, and ransoming.[22]

In today's world, *redemption* has lost some of that original meaning. We think of redeeming coupons or airline miles but not people. Part of this is for very good reason—redemption was closely connected to the slave trade in the ancient Middle East, and thankfully, slavery is no longer legal in most countries. When slaves were redeemed, they were delivered from bondage. In the most well-known example of this, God saved His people from Egypt and led them to the Promised Land.

Although we may not use the word *redemption* very often, it still describes a powerful part of who we are in Christ. Your redemption means you are delivered, ransomed, freed from bondage, and bought back. As a result, you belong wholly to God. The apostle Paul said, "It is for freedom that Christ has set us free. Stand firm, then, and do not let yourselves be burdened again by a yoke of slavery" (Galatians 5:1).

Freedom is ours because of our redemption, but it's up to us to protect that freedom and live it out each day. Unlike the little boat, we have a choice about following the currents that threaten to carry us away. We can flow in God's grace instead. He'll be there to guide us and keep us secure until our ultimate redemption in eternity.

You are redeemed.

Reflect

Read Isaiah 43:1-7. How would you define *redemption*? Redemption means that I…

What behaviors or lies most often keep you from embracing the freedom that is rightfully yours?

Describe a time when God gave you freedom from something or delivered you in some way.

Respond

Lord, I'm so thankful You have redeemed me. I value the freedom I have in You, and I ask for even more of it in this area of my life:

You're *redeemed*,
bought with a price, paid in full,
of great worth to the heart of God.
And all of those mistakes?
Those failures you fear?
They're taken care of too.
Ashes into beauty.
Mourning into joy.
Stumbles into solid ground.
Our God is the great Redeemer,
and nothing, no one,
is beyond His power to set free
and make new.

THIRTY

Victorious

*In all these things we are more than
conquerors through him who loved us.*

ROMANS 8:37

The term *friendly fire* describes a situation in which military personnel unintentionally cause harm to their own forces. This type of loss is especially tragic because it's unnecessary and makes victory even harder to attain. When we see it in the news, we shake our heads and wonder, "How could that happen?" Yet as battles rage within us, we often engage in our own internal friendly fire.

The Lord brought this to mind during a difficult week in my life. I was fighting a cold, pressing through a challenging season at work, and dealing with some personal issues in my life as well. One morning a dear friend invited me to pray with her. I shared my frustrations, and she said, "You're called to be a warrior."

Tears came to my eyes. "I know. But right now I'm just tired. I don't feel like fighting anymore."

My friend gently placed her hands on my shoulders

and began to pray for me. As she did, I sensed the Lord whispering to my heart. "I am for you. When you come against yourself, you side with the enemy." I knew instantly what those words meant. When I don't feel good or I get discouraged, I begin an inner barrage against myself. I launch lies—"You're not good enough. You're letting everyone down. You're a disappointment to God." Each word wounds my heart further until I feel utterly defeated.

At the end of the eighth chapter in Romans, Paul asks four important questions:

"If God is for us, who can be against us?"

"Who will bring any charge against those whom God has chosen?"

"Who is he that condemns?"

"Who shall separate us from the love of Christ?"

All these rhetorical questions have one correct answer: No one. But I often offer a different answer: Me. God has defeated our enemies, given us victory, and made us more than conquerors. But because of free will, we can still choose to be against ourselves. When we do so, we fight on the enemy's side—whether we realize it or not.

I still struggle with the friendly fire that sometimes rages within my heart. But I'm learning that in this too, God has promised me victory. I may be my toughest opponent, but God isn't giving up on me. He isn't giving up on you either. We may never fight a military battle or face the kind of persecution the early church endured, but we are still warriors in a battle for our hearts and minds. God will give us the love, grace, and courage we need to fully claim the victory that is already ours.

You are victorious.

Reflect

Read Romans 8:31-39. What lies try to defeat you? What's the truth?

What helps you live in grace and not be your own worst enemy?

How can you and God fight the battles you're facing together?

Respond

Lord, thank You in advance for the victory that is mine through You! I ask for Your help to fight this lie in my life:

You are a woman of strength—
more than a conqueror,
able to do all things,
a warrior and princess
in the kingdom of God.
You are called to fight,
to minister, to pray, to change the world.
The Lord has given you all you need
and made you all you need to be for victory.
So go forth, strong sister,
with a smile on your face,
a heart full of hope,
and a determination to never stop
until you receive every blessing
God has for you.

THIRTY-ONE

Pursued

This is love: not that we loved God,
but that he loved us and sent his Son as
an atoning sacrifice for our sins.

1 JOHN 4:10

From the time we are little girls, we dream of being pursued. Popular fairy tales reflect this idea. The prince carries Cinderella's glass slipper from house to house, searching for the woman he loves. Another royal young man awakens Sleeping Beauty with a kiss. Rapunzel lets down her golden hair to the man who has searched for her and will rescue her from the tower prison. We all seem to long for someone to seek us out and declare that we are loved.

Surely this desire is planted there by God Himself—the Ultimate Pursuer. In *The Sacred Romance*, Brent Curtis and John Eldredge write, "The Christian life is a love affair of the heart. It cannot be lived primarily as a set of principles or ethics. It cannot be managed with steps and a program...Our heart is the key to the Christian life."[23] Christianity is the only religion that believes God reaches down to us before we can even reach up to Him. Others focus on standards of behavior, rules, and making sure we are worthy. In contrast, "God demonstrates His own love for us in this: while we were still sinners, Christ died for us" (Romans 5:8).

God doesn't stop pursuing us once we belong to Him. Prince Charming may have stopped bringing Cinderella flowers or singing her love songs after the honeymoon. But God continues to show us His love every day through the beauty of the world around us, the blessings He sends, His comfort in difficult times, and a thousand other ways. He speaks to our hearts more often than we realize.

If God goes to all this effort on our behalf, what does He want in return? It's much less complicated than we make it. *He wants to be loved.* He longs for our hearts to respond to His. The Old Testament is filled with God lamenting over His wayward people who have broken His heart. We think God wants us to accomplish great works for His kingdom, change the world, or be the best Christians who ever lived. I can fall into that trap all too quickly. Yet when I am quiet and still, listening to the voice of my True Love, I often hear Him whisper, "I want your heart more than your hands."

Yes, obedience and faithfulness come naturally with love. Consider this analogy: Marriage is intended to be a reflection of the intimate relationship God wants with us. A marriage in which one spouse declares "I love you" but hurts or cheats on the other does not reflect God's desire. A marriage in which one person dutifully carries out the commands of another to earn approval is not what God has in mind either. God seems to have designed us for pursuit and response, give and take, a partnership built on mutual love and passion. He draws us to Himself, and we respond. He gives, and we receive. He seeks us, and we let Him find our hearts.

If you've been wearing yourself out trying to earn God's love, you can stop. Let your heart rest, listen for His voice, and when you hear it, respond. The glass slipper of God's love fits you perfectly, and He's waiting for you to receive it.

You are pursued.

Reflect

Read 1 John 4:7-12. How does it make your heart feel to know God pursues you?

What helps you receive God's love instead of trying to earn His approval?

Describe a few ways God has shown His love for you.

Respond

Lord, You are the God of the universe, and yet
You desire to know me and have my heart. Wow!
I want to respond to Your love by…

We want to be wanted.
Known.
Loved.
Cherished.
We want to know
our hearts are worth winning.
There's an answer to those questions…
it's been there since the beginning of time,
echoing through the ages,
ending with "It is finished."
It's the ultimate pursuit—
the Heart of Heaven coming to earth,
leaving everything,
stopping at nothing,
so you'd know there isn't anything
He won't go through
to get to you.

THIRTY-TWO

Covered

Blessed are they whose transgressions
are forgiven, whose sins are covered.

ROMANS 4:7

In my first devotional, *Rain on Me: Devotions of Hope and Encouragement for Difficult Times,* I shared a story about God's umbrella. It began when I read the book *Captivating* by Stasi Eldredge. In one part she challenges women to ask God how He's showing them His love. I initially balked at the question.

Finally, with a sigh, I silently asked, "Lord, how in the world are You showing me You love me right now?" In an instant the answer came. I gently sensed God say to my heart, "I'm walking through the rain with you, and I'm giving you My umbrella."

My mind flashed back to a day in college when an unexpected storm swept in while I was in class. I dreaded the long trek home. As I exited my classroom, I couldn't believe what I saw. My boyfriend, Mark (who is now my husband), stood waiting for me with a smile on his face and an umbrella in his hand. He had come to walk me through the rain. It's one of the sweetest and most loving things anyone has ever done for me.

Of course, the best part of the walk home that day was staying right beside Mark. Umbrellas aren't very big, and the closer you get, the drier you stay. It's the same way with God.

I know what it's like to want to run into the rain as fast as possible. I've done exactly that many times. But the sweetest moments in my journey have come when I've chosen to stay under God's umbrella and let Him wrap His loving arms around me.

In this story, the umbrella represented God's care during a difficult season of my life. But it applies to our sins and mistakes as well. Like an umbrella, God's love shelters us with the forgiveness and grace our hearts so desperately need. Sometimes we think, "God could never accept me as I am. I have to leave His umbrella and prove that I'm worthy." But trying to perfect ourselves is like trying to stop every raindrop from falling from the sky. It's impossible.

There are many reasons why it's hard for us to stay under God's umbrella of forgiveness. Pride can be like a rain jacket we throw on that makes us feel as if we can handle everything on our own. Fear of rejection by God can make us huddle in a corner, cold and shivering, rather than letting Him keep us dry. Lies we've been told, such as "Good Christians have it all together," can also make us simply pretend it's not raining at all. But God longs for us to draw near to Him and let Him do for us what we could never do for ourselves. The umbrella that covers us was purchased at a high price— the death of His Son—and nothing can take it away if only we'll receive it.

As the apostle Paul said, "Neither death nor life, neither angels nor demons, neither the present nor the future, nor any powers, neither height nor depth, nor anything else in all creation, will be able to separate us from the love of God that is in Christ Jesus our Lord" (Romans 8:38-39). God's umbrella of forgiveness and grace is enough to cover you now and forever.

You are covered.

Reflect

Read Romans 4:1-8. Are you under God's umbrella of grace, standing in the rain, or halfway in-between? Why?

What are some lies that could make it harder for you to receive God's forgiveness?

What's the truth your heart needs to hear?

Respond

Lord, I ask Your forgiveness for…and I receive
Your grace. Thank You for covering my sins with
Your amazing love. Amen.

Adam and Eve.
A Garden.
The fall.
And they hide.
We've been hiding ever since.
Then One comes along and says,
"Come here, let Me wrap My love around you.
I'll protect you from the cold.
I'll keep you secure.
All those sins, mistakes, and failures
are covered.
No more hide and seek of the heart.
You've been found forever."

THIRTY-THREE

Comforted

Praise be to the God and Father of our Lord Jesus
Christ, the Father of compassion and the God of
all comfort, who comforts us in all our troubles.

2 CORINTHIANS 1:3-4

During my counseling internship I helped facilitate grief support groups. On "story night," the members brought photos of their loved ones and told us about their lives. There were tears and (surprisingly) laughter as we shared. It felt like a sanctuary, like standing on holy ground where all of mankind has walked. These people have changed the way I write. I see their faces. I remember their stories. I carry each one like a gift entrusted to me.

I thought I handled our first story night just fine. But later that night, as I picked out my pajamas, I suddenly and unexpectedly burst into tears. The outburst of emotion caught me off guard, and I sat down on the carpet in a daze. What were these tears about? Where had they come from?

Then I realized those tears were from God's heart.

I thought about Jesus at the tomb of Lazarus. "Jesus wept" is the shortest verse in the Bible, and yet it speaks so much. I knew at that moment that God enters our sorrow. He grieves with us. He doesn't stand on the sidelines and give us clichés. He doesn't say, "Don't cry—you'll see them again one day." No, the shoulders of the God of the universe shook with sadness that day at Lazarus's tomb. His nose ran. His eyes were red. His throat was raw.

God is not afraid of grief the way we are. We tip-toe around it because it's messy, uncomfortable, unpredictable. It reminds us of our mortality. It opens our wounds. So we don't go there.

But not God. No, He'll be the first one to show up at grief group next week. He'll have His arms open and His compassionate eyes fixed on those broken hearts. He'll cry with them as He did with the mourners at Lazarus's tomb.

And the amazing, mysterious, beautiful part of it all is that He chooses me to be there too. My arms can be His arms. My tears can be His tears. My words (I hope and pray) can be His words. If you're looking for God's presence, enter the sorrow of another. As soon as we arrive, we always find He is already there.

I've also discovered that His comfort is not limited to the big losses in our lives. Second Corinthians tells us He comforts us in all our troubles. We're likely to look for Him in the tragedies or major heartbreaks. But He is also there for the everyday hurts we often try to handle on our own.

A harsh word stings our spirits…God is there.

A bad day threatens to discourage us…God is there.

A disappointment knocks the wind out of our sails…God is there.

No situation or circumstance is too large or small for Him. "Jesus wept," and He still weeps with us, walks with us, and offers our hearts the comfort we need each day.

You are comforted.

Reflect

2 Corinthians 1:2-10. What does the word *comfort* mean to you?

How do you need God to comfort you right now?

Describe a time when you felt God's presence during your sorrow or pain.

Respond

Lord, I praise You because You are the Father of compassion and the God of all comfort. I'm so glad Your comfort is available to me not only for the big losses of life but also for the little things that sometimes discourage me. Today I need You to comfort me about…

You with those tears in your eyes,
that heaviness in your heart,
that bad day hanging on your shoulder…
Will you let the arms of heaven hold you close
so He can whisper these words in your ear?
"Oh yes, I know about loss.
I know it's hard to live in this world.
I understand.
I count your tears.
I number your troubles.
I'm here with you, for you,
surrounding you
with comfort and peace
until you step into eternity,
where I promise to wipe every
tear from your eyes
and place a forever-smile on your face."

THIRTY-FOUR

Validated

No matter how many promises God has made,
they are "Yes" in Christ. And so through Him
the "Amen" is spoken by us to the glory of God.

2 CORINTHIANS 1:20

In the short and sweet film *Validation*, a parking attendant offers affirmation and encouragement to all who come to have their tickets validated. He expresses disarmingly wonderful sentiments, such as "You are great" or "You have amazing cheekbones." A long line quickly forms to see this man who is offering what we often crave most and get least—confirmation that we matter, we are special, and we can make a difference in the world. Eventually the parking attendant lands a job as a photographer because he can make people smile like no one else. When someone validates us, we light up from within.

The parking attendant did a wonderful job of validating others in simple ways, but there is Someone who does so on a much deeper level. God is the Ultimate Validator because what He says to us is always based on truth. It's not just a compliment or observation but rather the most powerful *yes* our hearts can hear.

God validates us in two important ways. First, He always says yes to the promises He's made to us. He does whatever He says He will do. He doesn't go back on His Word or change His mind. Sometimes our emotions, our flesh, or the enemy tries to invalidate what God has said. That's actually the tactic the enemy used in the Garden of Eden. He planted doubt when he posed the question, "Did God really say…?" to Eve. In a subtle way, he was attempting to undermine the truth. Whatever God has said remains valid forever. You can believe it, live it, and hold on to it no matter what happens or how you may feel.

Second, God validates our true identity. That doesn't mean He tells us everything we want to hear. But He does say yes to who He created us to be. Each of us comes into this world with a set of gifts, abilities, and characteristics placed there by God so we can accomplish His purpose for our lives. We may say no at times to who we really are out of lack of understanding, fear, or even disobedience. But God continues to affirm who He has made us.

There are also certain parts of our identity that we share with all Christians. For example, we are children of God who are loved, accepted, and chosen. God always validates that truth as well. Nothing can change who you are in Him.

In *Validation*, people were drawn to the parking attendant for the same reason many of us are drawn to anyone or anything that can affirm us. We long for approval and a sense of achievement. So we please people. We abuse substances. We take on too much work. Yet all of those choices only deepen our need. But in God's kingdom, validation is not an award to be earned but rather a gift to be received.

God is always willing for you to offer your heart to Him so He can say yes to all you are in a more meaningful way than you've ever experienced before.

You are validated.

Reflect

Read 2 Corinthians 1:18-22. What are some ways you sometimes try to earn validation from God or other people?

How would your life change if you received God's validation as a free gift instead?

What truth about your worth has God seemed to be speaking to your heart lately?

Respond

Lord, thank You for validating Your promises and truth in my life. Today I ask You to remind my heart that You say I am…

God says the deepest
YES
your heart can hear.
YES
to who you are,
to what you're called to do,
to all that's good and right and true.
Every other yes is just an echo
of the One who created you,
loves you,
calls you His own.
YES
is the word that started your story
and the one that will be repeated
for all eternity.

THIRTY-FIVE

Supported

When I said, "My foot is slipping," your
love, O LORD, supported me.

PSALM 94:18

At age 15, my grandmother became a wife. At 16, she became a mother. After raising her two children, Eula Armstrong took in three of her nephews and raised them as well. She cared for her mother, who lived to be 99, for more than ten years. Now as her husband, my grandfather, faces health issues, she faithfully takes time each day to sit by his side at a nearby nursing home. Even beyond our family, my grandmother lifts up, takes in, or watches over anyone who needs it.

Perhaps my grandmother so readily offers support because she has experienced it. When she married my grandfather, she dropped out of high school. In her twenties she renewed her commitment to Christ. Armed with her faith and a determination to make a difference in the world, she headed back to school and eventually received not only her bachelor's degree but a master's degree as well. She used her degrees to serve as a youth director, work at a home for abused children, and teach high school English. She often says with a smile, "I ended up teaching the two grades I missed when I dropped out. The Lord restores."

My patient and kind grandfather, her partner for more than 60 years now, offered support along the way. The two of them are examples of commitment through life's hard times. She also received endless support from the God who called her name as a young woman and never let her go. He stayed with her through all of the ups and downs. Just when a challenge seemed to be too great, His loving hand was there to steady her and help her take one more step.

We all have that kind of support from our heavenly Father if we'll only receive it. Yet many of us don't realize God supports us, or we misunderstand what His support means. God isn't like a doting parent who says, "I will support whatever you do." God loves us enough to withdraw His support from anything in our lives contrary to His will. If we choose sin or disobedience, God will not endorse that behavior. But when we are seeking Him, even if we struggle or stray, we can be sure that His loving hand is beneath us every step of the way.

God also supports who we are and who He has designed us to become. He saw the potential in my grandmother even when she was a teenage high school dropout. When others might have discouraged her, He fanned the flames within her until they became a shining light for Him. Whenever you pursue your mission and purpose, you can be certain you have God's support.

As my grandparents have shown me, true support is free, unmerited, and inspired by love. God promises that kind of support to each of us as His children now and always. Deuteronomy 33:27 says, "The eternal God is your refuge, and underneath are the everlasting arms." Or as pastor Mark Schatzman says, "You are secure in the grip of grace."

You are supported.

Reflect

Read Psalm 94. Describe someone who has been supportive of you.

In what ways has his or her support shown you more of God's heart for you?

In what situation do you most need God's support right now?

Respond

Lord, thank You for Your loving support. I pray You will help me see and comprehend it even more, especially when…

⁓

It may seem as if you're on your own.
But you've got everlasting arms beneath you,
love all around you,
grace to see you through,
and enough strength to make it too.
You're supported
in ways you can't see,
more than you know,
and the One whose heart
beats with love for you
will never let you go.

THIRTY-SIX

Helped

So do not fear, for I am with you;
do not be dismayed, for I am your God.
I will strengthen you and help you;
I will uphold you with my righteous right hand.

ISAIAH 41:10

When Ohio school officials posted a help-wanted ad for a position, they expected a few responses. Instead, they received an avalanche of more than 700 applicants and had to extend the deadline just to accommodate the demand. Perhaps what's most surprising is the position itself. The ad wasn't for a new teacher or principal—it was for a custodian.[24]

We also put out help-wanted ads in our lives. But we rarely receive the response the school did, particularly when we're looking for assistance with the dirty work that comes with our messy hearts. Our ad might read something like this:

Wanted—someone to bring hope, encouragement, and love to a fallen human being. Hours vary. No guarantee of compensation.

The details differ with each of us. I might need help with depression. You might need assistance recovering from a divorce. Perhaps someone else needs support in getting freedom from an addiction. Whatever it may be, we all long for someone to answer the ad written by our hearts.

Sometimes someone seems to apply. A romantic partner comes into our lives, and we believe all of our troubles will disappear. A new job promises to brighten the future. Another glass of wine chases away the sorrows for a little while. But in the end, we realize that whatever we thought would give us help has actually just contributed to the hurt.

Fortunately, there is Someone who does promise to answer the help-wanted ads of our hearts. God sees our need and responds. We may be suspicious at first. Surely the God of the universe has better things to do than mop away our tears and clean the sin in our hearts. Isn't He overqualified? Or we may be ashamed to let Him into the mess of our lives. What if He sees that corner of our hearts where dust has been gathering for years? How will He accept us if He finds that stain on the carpet of our minds? Yet God clearly and consistently says, "I will help you."

God's help is much like the manna He sent to the Israelites wandering in the desert. They didn't have a source of food, so God provided a breadlike substance for them to collect and eat each day. But there were a few guidelines for the manna. The people were to gather just enough for that day, and it could not be stored. In the same way, we are to go to God for our daily bread. His help is always for today, not tomorrow or the distant future. The school couldn't say to the custodian, "Just clean once, and that should last us the whole year." And we can't say to God, "Just help me now, and that should last for the rest of my life." Real help is moment by moment, personal, and fitted to our needs for that day.

If God had an ad, it wouldn't be for help wanted. Instead it would say, "Help given—every day, everywhere, to everyone who will receive it."

You are helped.

Reflect

Read Isaiah 41:8-20. List some ways God has helped you.

What keeps you from receiving His help at times?

What "manna" do you specifically need from God today?

Respond

Lord, I'm so thankful You're ready and willing to help me. I want to fulfill Your plan and purpose for my life. I humbly ask You to...

Hang in there, girl,
Press in, press on,
and never give up.
You've got what it takes
because you know the One who gives.
You've got everything you need
because you belong to the One who has it all.
He's got a plan for you, *and it's good*.
It will unfold step-by-step, day-by-day,
and His love will go with you all the way.

THIRTY-SEVEN

Touched

*A man with leprosy came and knelt before
him and said, "Lord, if you are willing,
you can make me clean." Jesus reached
out his hand and touched the man.*

Matthew 8:2-3

In ancient times, leprosy was one of the worst diseases
you could get. It ravaged the skin and caused permanent damage or death, and those with leprosy were
also considered unclean and forced to live apart from
the community. Alone and untouchable, a leper lived
with constant loneliness and pain.

Physical leprosy is no longer as common, and cures
are now available, but we can still relate to the leper's
feelings of being weak and unaccepted. And if leprosy
in the Bible is also intended to represent sin or loss, then
we've all been infected. A crisis, failure, or temptation
comes into our lives by choice or circumstance. Before
we know it, our hearts are ravaged, relationships shattered, and dreams torn apart. Others keep their distance

from us. They don't know what to say or what to do. We, in turn, withdraw and nurse our wounds silently. We think, "Maybe they're better off without me."

Yet somewhere deep inside us a longing remains. It's the first desire we ever felt. As newborns, we arrived in this world craving the touch of another. Only loving arms could soothe us. As children we whimpered, "Hold me" when we got hurt or the monsters under the bed seemed too real. We're grown up now, but a part of us still longs for touch—not necessarily physically, but in a way that is much deeper. We yearn for a touch to our hearts that says, "I see you as you are, and I choose to enter the messiness of your life. I love you enough to reach out to you. You are worth it."

In a moving scene from the Gospels, a leper says to Jesus, "Lord, if you are willing, you can make me clean." The next verse says, "Jesus reached out his hand and touched the man." The leper didn't ask for Christ's touch. Surely he imagined that Jesus would speak powerful words, wave His hands in the air, or perhaps tell him to offer a special sacrifice at the temple. But Jesus saw that after years of being isolated, the man had a deeper need. Only after Jesus first offers the gift of touch does He say, "Be clean!" and heal the man.

Jesus still stretches out His hand and lays it on the messy, broken places of our hearts. No sin is too great, no hurt is too deep, and no fear is too strong to keep His love away from us.

You are touched.

Reflect

Read Matthew 8:1-4. Is there anything in your life you're afraid might keep God away?

What do you want to share with Him about it today?

What's the truth about His unconditional love?

Respond

Lord, I'm amazed You're so willing to reach out to me. I need Your touch in my heart and life. I pray You will...

Those scars on your heart,
those sins and stains you hide
aren't enough to keep Him from you.
The One who washes your feet
washes your wounds too.
Can you feel His touch?
It's gentle, full of love,
healing what hurts,
mending what's broken.
He reaches out to you,
holds you, keeps you in His care.
Can you feel His touch?
It's always there.

THIRTY-EIGHT

Never Alone

*And I will ask the Father, and he will
give you another Counselor to be with
you forever—the Spirit of truth.*

JOHN 14:16-17

On my first day of kindergarten, I refused to let my mother take me to school. I dressed up in my new outfit, got my little bag, and stood by the curb to catch the school bus. It all seemed like a grand adventure, and I couldn't wait to take on the world. The ride to school went fine. I knew where I was going and how long it would take to get there.

The ride home was another story. The bus took a different route, one I was unfamiliar with, and by the time I reached the arms of my anxiously waiting mom, I was in tears. She gently comforted me until everything was okay again, just as she always did.

I have no doubt that if my mom could have gotten on that bus with me, she would have. She loved me enough to let me go that day, but I know her heart was with me every mile of the way. The reality is, no human can always be with us. Distance separates us. Divorce may divide us. And eventually death comes between even the strongest of bonds.

Sometimes, as it did for me that day, our isolation comes from a choice to be independent. I'm all grown up now, but I still tend to act a lot like that little girl on the first day of school. I think, "I can do this on my own. Just put me on the bus, God, and I'll make You proud!"

But unlike any human, God truly is always with us. When we become Christians, the Holy Spirit comes to live within us, and He will be with us forever (John 14:16). Sometimes it's difficult to feel His presence. A loss may numb us with grief or anger. A betrayal may make us build walls so high that no one can get to our hearts. The busyness of life may cause us to think God is waiting somewhere for us when we have time. Yet even in those moments, He is still there.

If God is always with us, then it's up to us to learn to live in His presence. The difficulty of doing so is nothing new. Brother Lawrence, a seventeenth-century French monk, determined that he would learn to acknowledge and embrace God even in the most ordinary of tasks.

We cannot escape the dangers which abound in life without the actual and continual help of God. Let us, then, pray to Him for it continually. How can we pray to Him without being with Him? How can we be with Him but in thinking of Him often? And how can we often think of Him but by a holy habit which we should form of it?[25]

The greatest difficulty is not convincing God to be with us. Instead, the challenge is for us to realize He is already there, release our independence, and learn to live in loving relationship with the One who has promised to share every bit of our journey.

You are never alone.

Reflect

Read John 14:15-21. What difficulty or disappointment have you tried to get through on your own?

Describe a time when you sensed God's presence with you.

How does your heart feel knowing that God will never leave you?

Respond

Lord, thank You for being with me right now as I read these words. Help me to become more aware of Your presence and intentionally live in it daily. I love the way You…

⁓

Hey you, in the middle of the busy,
in search of quiet, looking for peace.
You don't have to go anywhere to find it.
It's here, *right here.*
It has a name and a heart that
beats with love for you.
"Come to Me," He says, "I'll lift that burden,
carry that load, settle your soul."
He knows how to calm storms,
quiet hearts, bring peace to our lives.
That place your heart longs to go,
away from it all?
It's not as far as you think.
It's anywhere He is.
And the best part of all…
He's always with you.

THIRTY-NINE

Desired

I belong to my lover, and his desire is for me.

SONG OF SOLOMON 7:10

Octavio Guillen and Adriana Martinez pledged their lives and love to each other at the young age of 15. They made that promise a reality 67 years later. No one knows why they waited several decades to be wed, but doing so earned them the record for the world's longest engagement.[26]

Perhaps one of them had hesitations about the union. Octavia might have been in love with Adriana, but maybe she wasn't sure about him. Certainly he could have chosen someone else. No one would have faulted him for moving on with his life. But I'd like to believe he remained faithful to her all those years until he finally married his one true love.

The Old Testament story of Jacob and Rachel is another story of enduring love. Jacob fell in love with Rachel instantly, but his future father-in-law was concerned about propriety. He made Jacob work seven years in return for Rachel's hand in marriage. Then on the wedding night, he secretly switched Rachel with her older sister, Leah. The next morning a forlorn Jacob was told he would have to work another seven years for his beloved Rachel. Yet all of that time "seemed like only a few days to him because of his love for her" (Genesis 29:20). That story is a picture of desire—a longing so deep that no time is too long to wait, no distance too far to travel, and no price too high to pay.

If that leaves you wistfully longing for someone to feel that way about you, rest assured that Someone does. The Song of Solomon has often been described as a picture of Christ and the church. In it the beloved declares, "I belong to my lover, and his desire is for me." You are the object of God's affection. Isaiah 62:5 says, "As a bridegroom rejoices over his bride, so will your God rejoice over you."

I often write at a local café, and one morning a young man asked if anyone was sitting next to me. I replied that the seat was free. He settled in and began asking me questions. As our conversation progressed, we enjoyed a mutually respectful discussion about our differing beliefs. At the end he said, "But it's impossible for us to have a personal relationship with God. Christian men say that just to appeal to women because they want a romantic relationship in their lives."

A bit taken aback, I paused and thought about that for a moment. Then I replied, "Perhaps the reason our hearts long for romance is because our relationship with God is *the* love story—the one our hearts were created to be a part of for all eternity." He reflected on this for a moment, smiled, and nodded as if a little glimpse of truth had made its way to his heart. I believe we all long for intimacy because we were created for it.

Somewhere along the line this longing can get twisted and tangled. Perhaps we are abused. We get hurt. We find ourselves broken. We lock up our hearts and throw away the key. "Besides," we think, "no one wants me anyway." But there is One on the other side of our heart's door who never stops knocking. "You belong to me," He whispers, "and I will wait as long as it takes."

You are desired.

Reflect

Read Song of Solomon 7. How did your love story with God begin?

What are some ways God has recently shown you His love for you?

What truth does He want to whisper to your heart today?

Respond

Lord, the way You love me is a mystery. I pray
You will help me fully believe it's true and show
my heart...

⌒

You're wanted
just as you are—
the imperfections and beauty,
the mistakes and strengths.
God sees you completely,
knows you fully,
and calls you His own.
Can you sense the voice of heaven
speaking out above the crowds
that try to tell you who you are?
He's the One saying,
"I choose her.
She's the one I want—
now and always."

FORTY

His Forever

*Being confident of this, that he who began
a good work in you will carry it on to
completion until the day of Christ Jesus.*

PHILIPPIANS 1:6

The ceiling of the Sistine Chapel in Rome bears one of the most well-known works of art in history. Artist Michelangelo took four years to paint 12,000 square feet of space. Yet even this masterpiece began with one small stroke of a brush. As the days went by, the images on the ceiling looked more and more like those in the artist's mind.

Our lives are like the Sistine Chapel in many ways. God, the true Master Artist, works each day on the canvas of our hearts. We may look at ourselves and see only a confusing blend of colors, a few stray lines, and places in need of repair. Yet God can see the big picture. When we received Christ as our Savior, we became new creations. Yet like Michelangelo, God is continually bringing forth that identity day by day, stroke by stroke, and line by line.

Sometimes this makes us question whether what He says about us is really true. When He talks to us about who we are, He is able to see the complete work of art. Because we live in a fallen world, we see only part. That's why we must hold on to the words the apostle Paul wrote about God finishing the good work He started in us.

When we lose sight of that truth, we're tempted to pick up the paintbrushes ourselves. Just stroll through the aisles at a local bookstore, and you'll see titles like *Transform Yourself in Ten Days* or *Become a New You Now*. The world tells us that we should be the ones creating our identity. We are called to partner with God in the process, but He is the One doing the work because only He can truly see the vision. Our role is to simply listen and obey.

Imagine walking into the Sistine Chapel, picking up a brush, and altering the painting. You might think, "Michelangelo is so traditional, but the world wants something more contemporary. I'll just add another few strokes right here." This makes us shudder because of what it would do to such a priceless work of art, but we often do the same to ourselves.

Throughout this devotional journey, you've learned more about who you are in Christ and your relationship with Him. I hope you've caught glimpses of the masterpiece He is creating in you. When He looks at you, He sees not only who you are but also who you will be for all eternity. The Sistine Chapel existed in the mind of Michelangelo long before anyone else could fully see it. *God is completing His work in your life a little bit at a time, but it is already complete in His heart.*

In the middle of our noisy world, keep listening to the still, small voice deep within you that's always whispering, "In My heart you are…"

You are His forever.

Reflect

Read Philippians 1:1-11. What has God shown you about His heart for you?

How has your view of who you are changed?

How has your view of who He is changed too?

Respond

Lord, thank You for all You've shown me about who I am in You. I will always remember…

You are God's masterpiece—
started in His heart, formed by His hands,
and offered as a gift to the world.
Much more than a work in progress…
you're His good work.
What He started in you
will gloriously unfold for a lifetime
and be completed in heaven.
He sees beauty in you
because you're made in His image
and redeemed by His love.
It's true.
God says you are…
created, chosen, cherished, celebrated
His forever.

Connecting Your
Heart to God's

Y ou may have grown up in church all of your life. Or you may have never even stepped foot in one. Either way, God's heart is full of love for you.

And no matter what, Jesus extends this to you: "Here I am! I stand at the door and knock. If anyone hears my voice and opens the door, I will come in" (Revelation 3:20).

We all mess up in life, and sin acts like a bolt on the door of our hearts. Only we can turn the lock and let Jesus come in the way He promises. No matter what you've done, it's never too much or too late. "If we confess our sins, he is faithful and just to forgive us our sins" (1 John 1:9). Simply tell God you're sorry and ask for grace. He always gives it.

Forgiveness opens the door to our hearts. Then we can ask Jesus to truly be Lord of our lives. Doing so might sound something like this...

Jesus, I ask for Your forgiveness. Thank You for Your grace that now covers me. I give my life completely to You. All I am, all I have, is Yours. Amen.

From now on, you're eternally connected to Christ! He sees you through eyes of grace and will help you grow.

Once you've opened the door to God, no one can ever shut it. Even if you wander away, He'll always welcome you back. You belong to Him, and He belongs to you—for this life and forever in heaven!

Here's God's promise to you: "If you confess with your mouth, 'Jesus is Lord,' and believe in your heart that God raised him from the dead, you will be saved" (Romans 10:9).

Notes

1. Julianna Slattery, *Beyond the Masquerade: Unveiling the Authentic You* (Carol Stream, IL: Tyndale, 2007), 6.

2. Francine Rivers, *An Echo in the Darkness* (Wheaton, IL: Tyndale, 1994), 428.

3. Anita Singh, "Antiques Roadshow Memorable Moments," *Telegraph .co.uk*, October 14, 2008. www.telegraph.co.uk/news/news topics/celebritynews/3197627/Antiques-Roadshow-memorable-moments.html.

4. Max Lucado, *Cure for the Common Life: Living in Your Sweet Spot* (Nashville, TN: W Publishing Group, 2005), 2, 4.

5. Fil Anderson, *Running on Empty: Contemplative Spirituality for Overachievers* (Colorado Springs, CO: Waterbrook Press, 2004), 37.

6. Anderson, *Running on Empty*, 44-45.

7. Rolf Garborg, *The Family Blessing: Discover the Powerful Gift of Legacy and Life God Has Given You through Your Words* (Lakeland, FL: WhiteStone Books, 2008), 22-23.

8. Dorothy Still Danner, "Dorothy Still Danner: Reminisces of a Nurse POW," *Navy Medicine*, May/June 1992, 36.

9. www.sprinkles.com/about/food_philosophy.html.

10. John Piper, *Don't Waste Your Life* (Wheaton, IL: Crossway Books, 2010), 79.

11. Lucado, *Cure for the Common Life*, 42.

12. Bob Burns and Kevin O'Keefe, "The Average American," NPR, October 25, 2005. www.npr.org/templates/story/story.php?storyId=4973770.

13. Laurie Beth Jones, *The Path: Creating Your Mission Statement for Work and Life* (New York, NY: Hyperion, 1996), xviii.

14. Angela Thomas, *Do You Think I'm Beautiful? The Question Every Woman Asks* (Nashville, TN: Thomas Nelson, 2003), 18.

15. Cited in Whitney Hopler, "Discover Your Creativity," *Crosswalk.com*. www.crosswalk.com/spirituallife/1141906/.

16. "Friends for Seventy Years," *New York Times,* March 1, 1914. www.query.nytimes.com/gst/abstract.html?res=9807E3DC1E39E633A 25752C0A9659C946596D6CF.

17. Annabelle Meizel, "Friends 4-ever: 70 years and the closeness still grows," *Palm Beach Post,* December 25, 2008. www.palmbeachpost.com/shopping/content/accent/epaper/2008/12/25/a6d_ch45_friends_1225.html.

18. Janet Kornblum, "Study: 25% of Americans have no one to confide in," *USA Today,* June 22, 2006. www.usatoday.com/news/nation/2006-06-22-friendship_x.htm.

19. Roy Lessin, "Serving God in Your Place." www.dayspring.com/ad/mail/.

20. Brennan Manning, *Abba's Child: The Cry of the Heart for Intimate Belonging* (Colorado Springs, CO: NavPress, 2002), 59.

21. Donna Partow, *Walking in Total God-Confidence* (Minneapolis, MN: Bethany House, 1999), 83.

22. Cited in Walter Elwell, "Redeem, Redemption," *Baker's Evangelical Dictionary of Biblical Theology* (Grand Rapids, MI: Baker Books, 1996).

23. Brent Curtis and John Eldredge, *The Sacred Romance: Drawing Closer to the Heart of God* (Nashville, TN: Thomas Nelson, 1997), 8-9.

24. Arianna Huffington, "Ohio School Janitor Job Gets 700 Applicants," *The Huffington Post,* March 8, 2009. www.huffingtonpost.com/2009/03/08/ohio-school-janitor-job-g_n_172865.html.

25. Brother Lawrence, *The Practice of the Presence of God: The Spiritual Secrets of a Humble Brother Who Enjoyed Closeness with God* (Grand Rapids, MI: Spire Books, 2005), 51.

26. www.oddee.com/item_96837.aspx.

A note from Holley...

Thanks so much for reading *God's Heart for You*! As an author, speaker, and counselor, I love connecting with women through words. I wish I could take you out for a cup of coffee today. Until we get that chance, you're invited to stop by my place online at www.holleygerth.com. You can say hello, find out more, and even sign up for free encouraging e-mails from my heart to yours.

Meet you there!

❧ *Holley Gerth* ❧

More Great Harvest House Devotionals You'll Enjoy

One Minute with God for Women
Hope Lyda

Hope Lyda shares inspiration and spiritual nourishment in devotions created for your busy life. Along with Scriptures and prayers, this gathering of meditations provides the gifts of wonder and faith, deeper relationship with God, encouragement for tough stuff, and reminders of mercy and grace.

10-Minute Time Outs for Busy Women
Grace Fox

Grace Fox encourages you to make time for what matters most—your relationship with God. Her real-life stories and Scripture-based prayers will help you understand God's truth and apply it to everyday life.

A Woman's Path to Inner Beauty
Ginger Garret

Are you longing for inner and outer beauty? Join Ginger Garrett on a life-changing path to spiritual, emotional, and physical health. Biblical devotions, meaningful prayers, and practical beauty and faith steps inspire you to explore the transforming relationship between worshipping your Creator and caring for yourself.

Living God's Dream for You
Julie Clinton

The president of Extraordinary Women ministries shares devotions rich with wisdom gained through her ministry, life, marriage, and faith. Her message inspires you to grab hold of God's dream for you as you discover the depth of Jesus' love, the wonder of your worth, and the joy of walking in His purpose.

To learn more about other Harvest House books
or to read sample chapters, log on to our website:

www.harvesthousepublishers.com

HARVEST HOUSE PUBLISHERS

EUGENE, OREGON